Healing the Human Heart

Tools & Techniques for a Happy Life

NORMA CAMPBELL, MSW, MA

Disclaimer: The names and identifying characteristics of the people discussed in this book have been changed to protect their privacy.

PUBLISHED BY:
Norma Campbell
2629 Highway 70
Manasquan, NJ 08736
www.normalight.com

©2013 BY Norma Campbell

ALL RIGHTS RESERVED
NO PART OF THIS BOOK MAY BE USED OR REPRODUCED IN ANY MANNER WHATSOEVER, ELECTRONIC, MECHANICAL, PHOTOCOPYING, RECORDING, OR OTHERWISE WITHOUT THE PRIOR WRITTEN PERMISSION OF THE PUBLISHER

ISBN: 978-1-4675-4084-1

Cover and text design by Brian P. Mullen

PRINTED IN Florida

Please visit **www.normalight.com** for additional copies or to learn about our other products.

Volume discounts available.

Contents

Introduction

PART I: HEALING

Chapter 1	The Path to Healing	8
Chapter 2	How to Heal From the Past	29

PART II: CREATING INNER PEACE

Chapter 3	How to De-Stress Your Life	50
Chapter 4	How to Love Yourself	71
Chapter 5	Meditating Can Transform Your Life	86

PART III: CLAIMING YOUR HAPPINESS

Chapter 6	How to Be Happy	102
Chapter 7	Develop a Great Attitude	111
Chapter 8	How to Develop Your Intuition	121
Chapter 9	How to Be in Your Power	137

PART IV: MAKING ENJOYABLE CONNECTIONS

Chapter 10	How to Develop Satisfying Relationships	152
Chapter 11	How to Be a Giving Person	163

PART V: REWARDING LIFE'S ACTIONS

Chapter 12	Set Goals for Yourself	170
Chapter 13	Follow Your Heart's Desires	183
Chapter 14	How to Get Rid of Minor Annoyances	197

PART VI: LIVING A LIFE FILLED WITH JOY

Chapter 15	How to Get Rid of "Joy Squashers"	204

PART VII: LIVING A GOOD LIFE

Chapter 16	Develop an Attitude of Gratitude	240
Chapter 17	Ask for What You Want	251

Conclusion: Living an Extraordinary Life ... 261

Compliment Journal ... 262

Introduction

After experiencing a severe crisis, trauma, or loss, people often think that in time they will "get over it." Those who have experienced childhood trauma are even more likely to tell themselves that they are no longer suffering the effects of something that happened many years ago. These people—and they number in the millions—live lives of turmoil and drama. Only by developing tools and techniques to work through their feelings can they move beyond despair and hopelessness.

Experiencing a severe crisis, trauma, loss, or unresolved childhood feelings can make you feel as though it is the end of the world. It is not. I know first-hand how these things can negatively impact your life and make you feel a sense of hopelessness and despair, until you heal from that experience.

After my father committed suicide when I was fourteen, life was never the same. From that point on, I had to take care of myself. My mother was struggling financially, so I had to pay her rent. The day after my father died, I had full responsibility to pay for everything I needed and wanted, including my own food. I was terrified. I began working as a dishwasher and continued to work very hard throughout high school and college. My classmates at school often made comments that I worked too much.

I ran away at the age of fifteen and ended up living with an aunt, which only added to my sense of hopelessness and despair. It was only after a good friend confided to the school guidance counselor about my situation that my life began to turn around. That guidance counselor talked to me every week and encouraged me to go to therapy. At the age of seventeen, I was determined to do whatever it would take to heal from the trauma and loss in my past. What it took was being in therapy for five years, reading numerous self-help books, attending dozens of seminars, earning two master's degrees in counseling, learning to heal myself, and then helping my patients to heal. Now I offer the proven techniques that helped me and the hundreds of people I've counseled to finally move beyond their severe crisis, trauma, and loss to a joyous new beginning.

My own life was filled with total despair after my father committed suicide. Not having a place to live at times during my teen years and being on my own frightened me to no end. I never thought that I would graduate high school. The only thing that truly mattered to me was surviving in this world. It was only through my spirituality and my own healing that I was able to earn two master's degrees, travel extensively, open a successful private practice, have wonderful people in my life, and feel an abundance of joy and freedom. If I could go from living a life of total despair to living a life of joy, happiness, and freedom, then so can you!

After experiencing a severe crisis, trauma, or loss, you may think that you can bypass the healing process unscathed. People who have experienced childhood trauma are even more likely to tell themselves that they certainly cannot still be affected by what happened so many years ago. Their denial about how their childhood impacted them will only lead to a life of turmoil and drama. Meanwhile, as people hold on to their denial, they cannot understand why their lives are in turmoil and why they lack joy, motivation, and peace.

The answer is simple: they have not healed the negative impact that their childhood had on them. In order to be healed and live a happy life, they must work through feelings and develop the necessary tools and techniques that will facilitate this process. *Healing the Human Heart: Tools and Techniques for a Happy Life* will help you to heal emotionally and psychologically from your current and/or past difficult situations.

This book is based on my own healing process and on my sixteen years of experience being a psychotherapist and three years as a mental health consultant. *Healing the Human Heart: Tools and Techniques for a Happy Life* is about much more than healing. It is also about taking great care of yourself, creating freedom in every area of your life, developing satisfying relationships, following your heart's desires, and creating an abundance of joy.

With the tools and techniques offered in this book, you will not only heal but also develop deeper relationships and transform your negative thinking, beliefs, and actions into positive ones. I like to say that we are all capable of living an extraordinary life—one in which everything is working for us, we have freedom both emotionally and financially and are not weighed down by life, a peaceful, happy, healthy existence that we can enjoy, with a sense of purpose and good relationships. For people who haven't known this before, it means having a better life than ever. Read on to give these gifts to yourself.

PART I

Healing

CHAPTER 1

The Path to Healing

You did not experience your difficult situation just for the sake of it. There is a reason why this happened to you. If the person closest to you knew for sure that you were going to be brought to a whole new level of peace, joy, and happiness, but first you needed internal growth that only this difficult situation can offer, you would say forget it. You would try to convince that person and yourself that your life is just fine the way it is. You would rather live a mediocre life than have to go through any form of temporary suffering. I do not blame you! It is much easier to live a mediocre life than to heal. When you are experiencing deep emotions, you may have trouble believing that there is something great in store for you and that your pain is the catalyst that will start you in the right direction.

The good news is that there are greater things in store for you! You are not meant to live a mediocre life. You are meant to live an extraordinary life filled with great joy and peace. You are completely capable of healing. As the saying goes, "You will not be given more than you can handle." You may feel at this moment that you cannot handle your difficulties, but you can.

Keep in mind that through suffering comes the greatest growth. It is not easy for a loving parent to let a child ride her bike for the first time, without training wheels. You know that she is likely to fall, scrape her knees, and cry. It is not easy for loved ones to see you fall and cry because of your hardships. However, this is a necessary part of growing and evolving. Once you are living an extraordinary life, you will no longer focus on the fact that you were once hurting terribly. Just like a child who grows up will no longer focus on the times when her knees were bleeding every time she fell off her bike. This will be a memory that no longer hurts.

The healing process is similar. You will remember your difficult situation; however, once you are healed, that deep cut of yours will become a scar. Look at a scar that you currently have. Does that scar hurt you? Of course not! When you feel your feelings, your emotional wounds are in the process of becoming healed. As you start to heal, you will begin to develop a scar. When you do not feel your feelings, your wound will remain open. Every time a difficult situation comes your way, you will have a strong reaction, as though salt were being poured on your wound.

When you "stuff" your emotions by keeping them unexpressed, you will also experience the heaviness of your feelings. It can be exhausting to carry an emotional backpack throughout life. Perhaps you have been carrying this for years. You cannot be at peace when you are carrying a heavy emotional backpack and keeping your wounds open. You can choose to stuff your feelings, carry all that weight around and keep your wounds open, or you can choose to fully heal. Why not get rid of your emotional backpack and heal your wounds? Once you heal, not only will you have great joy, peace, and happiness, but you will also have the pleasant experience of seeing that what once caused you great agony will no longer affect you at all. The salt will simply fall off your arm since your wound will be healed. No more stinging for you!

If you choose to fully heal, then your suffering will be temporary. IT IS MUCH EASIER TO EXPERIENCE TEMPORARY SUFFERING THAN TO LIVE A LIFE OF MISERY! Again, your suffering is temporary. The wonderful thing about being healed is that you will be free from ongoing turmoil. You will react more positively to every situation that occurs. Rather than let things bother you and fester, you will take the necessary action in order to remain in a peaceful state. The journey toward becoming healed will require patience on your part. Be patient and allow your intuition to ultimately guide you along the way.

"One of the secrets

in life is to make

stepping stones out of

stumbling blocks."

— Jack Penn

There will be times when you feel all alone and as though your situation is never going to change. When this occurs, as a result of a major crisis, trauma, or loss, you are going through what I call "the tunnel." The healing process can be very difficult and painful. Even if you are healing from early childhood trauma or loss, you may be thrown in the tunnel.

This process lasts much longer than simply having a black cloud hanging over your head. With black clouds, an upsetting situation or your feelings may change very quickly, where you see the sunshine again and feel good. With the tunnel, you have to take one step at a time without ever knowing exactly when you will see the light. This is because you are going through a major healing and growth process. Believe me, YOU WILL SEE THE LIGHT AGAIN! Even after you start to see the sunshine and life feels good, you may still have more healing to do before you are fully free from the impact of your situation. Keep moving forward knowing that each day you are a step closer to this goal. If you are not in the tunnel, be grateful! You may still have healing to do; however, you will be able to heal at a much gentler pace.

Many people have been terribly wounded at some point in their lives. You may be wondering how you will know if your wounds are healed and you are living the life you were meant to live. If you can honestly answer yes to all of the following questions, then you have accomplished that goal. Wherever you answer no, this means that you have some more work to do. When you start to feel good again, you may want to revisit this list to see what areas in your life need more attention.

Are you living a life of peace and joy?
Is your life working for you?
Are you grateful for all of the good that is in your life?
Do you always listen and follow your intuition?

Are you able to fully assert and take care of yourself?

Do you really like and love who you are?

Are you living a fun, enjoyable life?

Are you fulfilling your life's purpose?

Are you a kind person?

Do you have a great attitude about life?

Do you trust the process of life, without living in fear, even when facing adversity?

Are you authentic in all of your interactions with people?

Are you able to easily express your thoughts, feelings, and ideas?

Are you pursuing your heart's desires?

Do you enjoy all of your relationships?

Have you let go of the past, so that it no longer negatively impacts you?

How many yeses do you have? Which areas of your life still need work? If you answered no to all the questions, do not worry. This simply means that you are in great need of healing. There are many people who will also answer no to every question. You are not alone!

From being a psychotherapist for many years, I get great pleasure out of helping people to change their "no's" to "yeses," so that they can fully enjoy their lives. It has been a wonderful experience for me to see people's "no's" become "yeses." Many of my patients throughout the years have been in awe by how great life can be as a result of healing, being in their power, and developing their spirituality. This can happen to you, too, if you allow it!

As you heal, it may seem as though your suffering will never end. It may take some time, but I assure you it will! Repressed emotions from childhood are also likely to surface during a new crisis, trauma, or loss, which makes things more difficult. Getting through your current situation is already difficult enough without having to heal unresolved feelings from the past. At times, you may feel that it is nearly impossible to get through this difficult time, but you will!

Your difficulties are further compounded when your loved ones know that you are in the tunnel, but they are unaware of the daily struggles that you face as you blindly walk through the darkness. The last time loved ones remember seeing you, as they kissed and hugged you good-bye, you were just entering that dark place with your survival tools. As time goes by, loved ones will move on with their lives and you will be left with figuring out a way to make it through that uncomfortable place, while wishing and hoping that you will soon see the light.

What people do not realize is that you may be suffering even more as time passes, since you feel scared and alone. There will be days when you feel as though you are completely alone as you walk and sometimes crawl through that dark, cold, smelly tunnel. Keep in mind that every experience that you have is for a reason. We sometimes need to experience great turmoil in order to grow into being the person we were meant to be, so that we can fulfill our life's purpose.

How open are you to healing and growing? Are you afraid to grow because this can be uncomfortable at times? It takes a very brave person to heal through difficult situations that have left scars. You are that brave person! You just may not know it. Our world needs you to heal. We are counting on you to be the person you were meant to be. Just think, you have a whole world of friends who are silently cheering you on to become the person you were meant to be. With the current conditions of our world, it is imperative that we silently cheer you on. We need your light and love to help this planet. One person can make such a grand difference in people's lives. You were meant to impact this world positively, even if on a small scale. I know that it can be challenging to be who you are meant to be when life has beaten you down. I have experienced this myself. However, the rewards that come from being healed will certainly be worth all of your efforts to get there!

> *"The best way to predict your future is to create it."*
> *— Stephen R. Covey*

Carol experienced great suffering as a result of the death of her mother, her divorce, and from financial difficulties. As soon as she found out that her husband had been cheating on her for many years, she was convinced that her life was never going to be good again and that there was not much to live for. After her best friend encouraged her to seek professional help, she called me. Carol wanted a magical cure when she first started seeing me for counseling. I let her know that unfortunately there was no magical cure and that her healing would take time.

In therapy, Carol was fully committed to working through her losses. She allowed herself to feel all her feelings and began to listen to her inner voice for the first time in her life. In the course of her two-year treatment, her social life blossomed when she met people from yoga class, hiking trips, and dance classes. Toward the end of our work together, Carol said that she was happier than ever! If someone would have told Carol that her life would be better than ever once she was out of the tunnel, she NEVER would have believed them. After I mentioned to Carol that I was writing a book, she asked me to please let everyone know that "THEY WILL GET THROUGH THE TUNNEL AND THAT LIFE CAN BE BETTER THAN EVER ONCE YOU HEAL!"

As you heal, people will be sent in your life to help you. If you need more support, do not be afraid to seek it. The more support you have, the easier it will be to see those glimpses of light, which will help along the way. When you are forced into the tunnel like a blast of wind from a tornado, you will also need much comfort. This will make those dark days not seem so dark. It is important to give this to yourself as much as you can. Healing through past or present wounds can be very scary at times. Stay focused on the white light that is within you. This white light will guide, comfort, and help you.

You may feel as though you are walking through your healing process as slowly as a caterpillar. Yet, before you know it, you will have beautiful wings that will help you to soar. As you soar, you will freely enjoy the life you were meant to live. This is one of the gifts that we get for our hard work. Healing, growing, and evolving can be uncomfortable at times, but wait until you see the color of your wings!

> *"When written in Chinese, the word 'crisis' is composed of two characters. One represents danger and the other represents opportunity."*
> *— John F. Kennedy*

Losing a child is one of the worst losses that anyone can experience. For the patients I have seen who experienced this unthinkable loss, the pain they endured throughout their healing process was absolutely heart-wrenching. The amazing thing is that once these people were out of the tunnel, their perspective on life and the way they lived their lives had completely changed. Their incredible loss helped them to see what was really important in life and to live life to the fullest. Ron, who lost his daughter when she was twenty-five, told me that he learned to "Never sweat the small stuff in life." He also said that "Little things do not matter." He realized that his daughter would have wanted him to be happy. Instead of letting his daughter's death destroy his life, Ron decided to appreciate each and every day. Ron knows that life is precious. He is now helping to feed poor people around the world. Ron mentioned that the foundation that he started in his daughter's memory makes him feel good. This has been the one thing that helped him to move forward. What will help you to move forward?

As you work toward becoming healed, take one step at a time on this journey, regardless of how long it takes. There may be times when you do not feel like taking one more step forward in your healing process. You are not alone in your struggles. Millions of people are walking in their tunnels, as you walk in yours. Keep focusing on the thought that what you are going through is temporary. Think of the last tunnel that you drove through. You may have felt as though you were never going to exit that uncomfortable place, but you did. The same is true now. You may feel that you are going to be suffering forever, but you will not. Your inner light will guide you toward taking baby steps forward, so that you can soon embrace inner peace. Even if you are not in the tunnel, it is important to take one step at a time and remind yourself that your situation is temporary.

One of the most challenging things to do while you are healing is to trust that there is a good plan for your life. When you do not trust, you are creating more turmoil for yourself. Your lack of trust then becomes a major block and you are left with feeling even more scared. When you trust, even in your darkest moments, this will free you from being stuck in the mud. You cannot move forward if you are stuck.

One of my dearest friends, Pam, refused to trust because she had suffered from tinnitus. The nonstop ringing in her ears, caused from tinnitus, severely depressed Pam for two years and created a negative ripple effect, so that she was unable to sleep for more than a couple of hours each night. She could barely function at work and in life. Her health started to decline in other ways as a result of the stress and emotional suffering that the constant ringing caused. Pam even considered taking her own life. At that point, she refused to trust and believe that she would be okay; therefore, she made it very difficult for her intuition to guide her. You may feel too angry to even think about trusting that you will be okay, too. Once you release your anger, you can work on one of the most important tools that you need to have: trust.

Once Pam began to trust, she started to listen to her intuition and she did exactly what she intuitively knew that she needed to do. After Pam listened, and took action, 99 percent of the ringing in her ears completely stopped! As a result, Pam was able to sleep well, feel better, and soar in life. Pam said that working out was the one thing that helped her the most! Pam's whole attitude was forever changed as a result of her being in the tunnel. She is now very happy, positive, and excited about life. When I reminded Pam a few years ago how far she had come, she replied with an upbeat, enthusiastic voice, "There is a good reason for our suffering." Pam's suffering helped her to live in the moment and enjoy life, without fear.

You can bet that you are going to benefit from healing. Some of these benefits may include: feeling good about yourself, enjoying life more than ever, developing your spirituality more than ever, moving through life with confidence, and relying on your inner wisdom. When Pam was experiencing trauma, her father flew from Taiwan to New York to be with her. Pam had not seen her father for several years. He was more positive and encouraging than he had ever been to her. He told her to remain positive and to expect a miracle. He even offered to pay for her to join a local gym. That was the first time in Pam's life that her father had ever been so generous. As a result of her suffering, she not only grew much closer to her father, but she also became a woman who was no longer afraid to live life fully. She now volunteers often, travels, and takes risks that she never dreamed of taking before she got tinnitus. She is also more determined than ever to live an extraordinary life!

No matter where you are in your process, make a commitment to do whatever it takes to become healed, so that you can live an extraordinary life. The more determined you are to live this kind of life, the easier it will be to move forward when there are bumps in the road. No matter what you are going through, someone has gone through something similar, healed, and soared, and so can you!

The uncomfortable feelings that you are now experiencing will end when you are healed. Many of my patients who have gone through a severe crisis, trauma, or loss at one point felt as though their pain was never going to end and that they were going to live a life of misery. As a result of their healing, they came to realize that this was not true. Toward the end of their treatment, most of these patients stated that they were happy overall. When I first started counseling these individuals, they never would have believed that they could have experienced any happiness after what they had gone through. We are not meant to be miserable. We are meant to heal, grow, and evolve, so that we can live a great life of peace and joy!

Good things often come out of suffering. You may have a greater appreciation for life and humanity as a whole. The strength, insight, and clarity that you will gain as you heal will positively impact you. As you continue to heal, you may discover that you are more determined than ever to be happy and peaceful. All the pain you have felt has brought you to this very moment of being on the healing journey. Good for you! Most people need to experience deep pain before they make a commitment to become healed and happy. Yes, it is unfortunate that life works this way, but this is reality.

If we did not suffer enough, then we would not even realize that something was missing in our lives. When you are healed, you will see how amazing you are! You will become fully aware of the strength and power that is within you. No one will be able to persuade you into deception when you are fully in your power. Being healed will make you into a person who is strong, powerful, confident, loving, kind, compassionate, giving, and a light in this world. Stop feeling sorry for yourself and focus on the good that will be yours for moving beyond the rubble that you were under. The truth is that most of us on earth have suffered in one way or another. Take this suffering and turn it into greatness by becoming healed and doing what you are meant to do.

When you are healed, it is almost as though you have a trampoline inside of you from which hurtful things bounce off you quickly. When you have major healing to do, the trampoline is pushed to the side and you are in a hole. It may seem as though the hole keeps getting deeper every time you go through more difficulties or you feel rejected.

If you decide to stop healing when you have more work to do, then you will be settling for a mediocre life. The choice is yours. The peace and joy that comes from being healed will be greater than any peace and joy that you have ever experienced in your life! This joy will impact every aspect of your being: body, mind, and spirit. Many people believe that acquiring great wealth and success is the key to life. Acquiring great wealth and success will not guarantee that you will be happy and peaceful, but being healed will!

> *"There can be no transforming of darkness into light and apathy into movement without emotion."*
> — *Carl Jung*

One of the most difficult, yet necessary, things to do is to feel your feelings. This is a natural part of being human and a requirement in order to heal. You can pretend that you are not even impacted by your current situation or past trauma or loss, but you are only fooling yourself. All you are doing is suppressing your emotions. New situations will continue to occur in your life that will tap into those old feelings and make them come out.

If you experience enough difficulties in life, your stuffed emotions will begin to surface and you will be forced to examine them. You will then have to stop pretending. It is much easier to give in to these emotions, rather than have life present difficult situations that will elicit those emotions. If you are not sure whether you tend to stuff, then the chances are that you do. If you are truly aware of what is going on in your internal world, then you will consciously be aware of your emotions at all times.

If you have been in the habit of stuffing, then you may not know how you truly feel at any given moment. Perhaps you are numb on the inside because you refuse to deal with your emotions.

People who continue to stuff their feelings will live a life of turmoil and unhappiness. How do you stuff your feelings? Are you doing this by medicating them with food, alcohol, drugs, or some other addictive behavior? If so, feeling is scary for you. Many people worry that they will not cope with life if they feel. If your feelings overwhelm you to the point where you cannot function or you are depressed, seek professional help. Find a good therapist or pastor who can guide you on your journey toward becoming healed. There is nothing wrong with having someone help you through your healing. In fact, many people benefit from professional help. There is nothing weak about receiving help. On the contrary, it takes a very strong person to work through difficult emotions.

Susan's journey toward becoming healed began the day she stepped into my office at the young age of nineteen. Her life felt completely hopeless and out of control when she began therapy. Looking back, Susan said that being in therapy was one of the greatest decisions that she ever made. Her childhood was filled with great despair and hopelessness. In order for her to work through the incredible pain, anger, and shame from being severely abused as a child, she needed much support and help. Therapy was the one thing that helped her to heal and create a good life. To this day, Susan is grateful that she went for help. Her siblings who suffered similar abuse during childhood were not open to seeking help.

Today, their lives are filled with drugs, abusive relationships, self-hatred, and constant financial struggle. Susan knows that her healing has allowed her to be on a very different journey from that of her siblings. It took Susan several years to get where she is today. She put herself through college, opened her own business, and is now living the life of her dreams. She has a loving husband, two children, great friends, and a career that she loves. Her commitment to heal has paid off! She feels great about herself and life. She is a living example of how you can go from being severely abused as a child to becoming happy and healed.

Your healing will begin when you process your feelings in healthy ways. One of the healthiest ways to process your feelings is simply by being present to them and feeling them. You can also process feelings by calmly talking, crying, writing, exercising, meditating, and creatively expressing yourself through painting, drawing, music, and other creative pursuits. How do you process your emotions in healthy ways? You do not need to hold on to any unpleasant feelings. This will only stop you from being peaceful. Peace can only reside within you when you make room for it.

Most people are too scared to feel. Therefore, they miss the opportunity to heal. They think, "What is the use, there is too much garbage on the inside. It will be better if I continue to numb myself." They will then do whatever it takes to remain numb. They would rather ignore the mess that is inside than clean that big mess up by healing. The good thing is that you can start the healing process by simply taking a few minutes each day to feel. You certainly do not have to blast through as many feelings as possible. That would be exhausting. It is completely healthy to process things slowly. People are so terrified to deal with their emotions because it is uncomfortable to feel ugly feelings. Stuffed feelings, negative beliefs, negative thinking, negative actions, and dry spiritual wells are the ugliness that stop people from living a peaceful life, not feelings.

Throughout my healing process of many years, I learned not to resist my feelings. I decided when I was seventeen to fully allow myself to experience all my emotions. I intuitively knew that I would be better off healing than having to go through life being miserable on the inside. At that point in my life, I had enough misery. I was ready to experience a new path in life filled with love, peace, and joy. Believe me, throughout the years, I have felt some absolutely horrific feelings as a result of past trauma and loss. However, I am glad that I continued to feel those feelings and heal so that I could be where I am today.

It is important to process all your feelings, not just the ones that are easy for you to experience. Experiencing the positive emotions such as joy, peace, excitement, love, happiness, fulfillment, and passion are certainly wonderful to savor. However, you need to process the unpleasant feelings such as sadness, anger, shame, fear, loneliness, worthlessness, not feeling good enough, and so on, so that you can hold on to more of the good feelings. Yes, it can be very uncomfortable to process unpleasant feelings. However, the more you allow yourself to process them, the closer you are to becoming healed.

When you are feeling emotions that are difficult for you to feel, writing can help you to release those emotions. In order to process your feelings via writing, simply write what you are feeling and thinking. Keep writing until those feelings are fully released. You may need to write one, two, or fifteen pages of your thoughts and feelings. The more you write, the more you will be permanently releasing. After you write your feelings on paper, if you do not want anyone to read what you wrote, destroy it. Write as much as you need. Keep doing this process until you enter a peaceful state. Very often when you release feelings that you have been holding on to for years, or even some recent feelings, you may feel empty on the inside. It is important to fill this space with self-care and self-love. Make it a priority to do something nurturing for yourself after you write, such as taking a bath, listening to your favorite music, or going for a walk in nature.

There may be days when you wake up in the morning and you experience deep sadness. You may say to yourself, "How can this be? I thought I already experienced enough sadness." Not true! There is more to go. When you give in to your emotions, by feeling them, they will begin to dissipate. When was the last time you felt your feelings, without ignoring them? Whenever you feel, see a candle within you permanently burning away any emotions that are ready to be released. The more you feel, the more that candle will powerfully destroy any darkness that lies within.

The one emotion that is the most difficult for women to feel is anger. Women are taught as young girls that they are not allowed to experience this emotion. We all have felt angry at some point. If you are uncomfortable with anger, then remind yourself that stuffing this feeling is not healthy.

There may be a part of you that is too uncomfortable processing anger because it is "bad" to be angry. The bad thing about anger has to do with dealing with this emotion in destructive ways. Keep in mind that if you deal with this emotion in healthy ways, your depression is likely to decrease.

Children will model what they see. If a child sees a parental figure deal with anger in destructive ways, then this child is likely to model the exact behavior. Some destructive ways of dealing with anger include being verbally and emotionally abusive, physically hurting someone or yourself, destroying property, reckless driving, medicating anger with any addictive behavior, such as drinking or doing drugs. Nothing good comes from expressing anger in any of these ways. If you have dealt with this emotion in unhealthy ways, then realize at this moment that you can make better choices. The better choices that you can make for processing anger include calmly talking, exercising, meditating, being in nature, doing art work, punching a punching bag, popping a balloon or bubble wrap, and writing an anger letter.

Anger Letter

Anger letters are very powerful. The way to begin writing an anger letter is by giving yourself permission to write whatever comes to mind, without judging or shaming yourself for what you need to release on paper. In this letter, be sure to fully express why you are angry, who or what has angered you, and whatever else you need to say in order to release that emotion. Immediately after you write your letter, rip it up in tiny pieces so no one would ever be able to read what you wrote. You may also burn the letter. You can get a piece of aluminum foil and shape it into a little boat. Put the letter in the middle of the foil, then burn the ripped-up letter. It is best to do this somewhere safe outside. Be sure to water down your letter after you have nothing but ashes left. After you process your anger via writing, make sure that you nurture yourself for the exact amount of time that it took you to write the letter. If it took you one hour to write your letter, then you owe yourself one hour of nurturing time. Do not put this off until the next day. It is necessary to nurture yourself immediately after you write your anger letter. You may want to listen to soothing music, take a bath, or get a massage.

It is important to slowly allow yourself to feel. Keep in mind that all your feelings will not flood out at once; if they did, then NO ONE would choose to heal. Keep focused on the truth that you are NOT going to feel all your feelings at once. That is impossible! You may have some deep emotions come up from time to time, but this is temporary. There is no perfect formula for healing. Your way of healing is going to be unique because you are unique. If you need to cry, then cry. There will be times when your environment will not support you with releasing your feelings; you may be at work, at a social function, or with your in-laws for the weekend. If that happens, make it a point to release those emotions whenever you can.

If you are ever overwhelmed by your feelings, then it is time for a break. You do not have to feel every second of the day. There will be times when you say to yourself, "Forget it, I do not want to feel anymore. I have had it with this healing process. I do not care if I am ever healed." Take a break at that point. When you are ready, you can continue to process more.

Most people will be exhausted at one point or another throughout their healing, so you are not alone.

If someone makes you feel bad for feeling a certain way, remind yourself that you have a right to experience all your emotions. In fact, one of the healthiest things that you can do is to feel your feelings. Most people who try to make you feel bad have not dealt with their inner worlds. It is easier for others to try to get you to ignore your inner world, so that you stop stirring up theirs. How many times has someone said to you, "Do not feel that way"? You were being told that you were wrong for having your emotions. If you have gone through a major crisis, trauma, or loss, you will have MANY emotions that need to be felt. Claim your right to fully feel everything as you heal!

Throughout the healing process, you are going to experience a whole range of emotions. Don't let yourself feel wrong for having this range of emotions. Keep focused on the idea that there is nothing wrong with how you feel. The important thing is to just do it, without acting out your feelings or running away from them.

CHAPTER 2

How to Heal from the Past

Have you ever felt that your life simply will not work for you no matter what you do? This may be the result of carrying around wounds from the past. You cannot be free from the past until you heal these wounds. It will take time to heal, but you will get there. All you need to do is make a commitment to become healed, so that you can allow your intuition to guide you along the way. There will be times when this new journey will offer pleasant surprises. You will connect with people who are like-minded and in this way develop lasting friendships. Your connection with people will add to your life. You will no longer have the "poor me" attitude. Instead, you will have an attitude of victory and determination! This attitude will help you to make your heart's desires a reality.

If you have been abused or deeply hurt, it is imperative that you heal your wounds. If you do not, then the opportunity to do so will continue to present itself. At first, you may be spiritually pinched into seeing that you have some work to do. A spiritual pinch occurs when a situation comes your way to elicit feelings. For example, you may continue to be anxious every time you encounter a particular situation. Most people who are anxious do not even realize that they feel this way because of unresolved feelings. As time goes on, your anxiety will start to increase. You may suddenly discover that not only are you anxious about traveling, but now you are anxious about other things, too. As you continue to ignore the pinches, they will turn into spiritual punches. That is life's way of saying, "Excuse me, either work on healing now or you will get a stronger spiritual punch in the future. If you ignore the next spiritual punch, then there will be another one on the way." If you are anxious and you do not heal the underlying feelings that created the anxiety, then you are likely to see an increase in your anxiety. Your anxiety may be the catalyst that brings up childhood pain that was never felt. For others, a difficult situation may be the catalyst to do this. Choosing to heal is well worth not being stuck in the past and having to face many spiritual punches. It also better to work through the feelings that are the underlying cause of your anxiety, so that you can significantly decrease your anxiety.

A recent crisis, trauma, or loss can also powerfully stir up unhealed past issues. If your life is going along just fine, then you certainly are not going to say to yourself, "Gee, I have some healing to do since my childhood was not good." You may, however, be presented with the opportunity to heal the past after an incredible loss. You may ask yourself, "How will I know whether I am facing emotions from the past and not the present?" One way to identify whether or not a current situation is tapping into old feelings is by your reaction. If you have a much stronger reaction than what the situation warrants, then you are tapping into unfelt feelings from the past. An example of this would be if you are devastated when someone you barely know passes away. Your strong reaction to this loss is tapping into an earlier loss that you did not fully feel.

This is exactly what happened to me years ago. After I found out that my professor, Dr. B, passed away just two days after I had seen him, I could not stop crying. Even though Dr. B had a special place in my heart, my reaction to his loss was tapping into some of the grief that I did not fully feel from my father's death. At first, I could not believe how much grief I had over my professor's passing. A counselor at school who heard me crying in the hallway after a professor announced this shocking news to the class asked me if my father had passed away. She knew that I was feeling some of the sadness that I never fully felt from this earlier loss. Do not make yourself feel you are wrong for processing old feelings when a new situation brings them to the surface. Simply give yourself time to work through them.

The one common thing that my patients who were abused or experienced childhood losses said to me is that they felt as though they had a knot in their stomachs. As we worked on healing the reason why they started seeing me for counseling, we also unraveled old childhood feelings that were at the center of this knot. Have you ever felt that you have had a knot in your stomach? Perhaps this knot is the result of having repressed childhood feelings that you did not work through.

You may be thinking that you cannot be free from the past since you have been through so much. That is not true! Or you may wish that you could be instantly fixed. The healing process does not work that way. If you were negatively impacted during childhood, then it will take time to heal. It will take as long as it takes.

If you did not get good, healthy parenting while you were growing up, then you must re-parent yourself in order to get what you originally needed, but did not get. A loving parent would speak to you kindly, praise you often, give you much comfort, encourage you, and nurture you. This is your new job! If your parents constantly put you down and gave you negative messages, you need to encourage yourself. Say to yourself, "I know I can do this, since I have this desire in my heart. I have everything it takes to make this happen. All I need to do is take one step at a time as I work toward my heart's desire. I can do it." How can you encourage yourself at this very moment? Make it a daily practice to be a loving parent to yourself, regardless of your age. If you are beating yourself up in any way, then you are not being a loving parent to yourself. You may think that it is silly to speak lovingly to yourself, but it is actually empowering and beneficial.

Wounded adults often attract wounded partners. The partner then becomes the mother or father figure in the relationship. On some level, they are trying to get the good parenting they never received; however, this will only lead to a parent/child relationship. It takes two whole individuals to make a healthy relationship, not two wounded people. Even though it feels good to have others meet some of your needs and nurture you, it is your responsibility to meet a great majority of your needs and be that good parent to yourself.

How often are you kind, nurturing, and loving to your inner child? When was the last time you bought yourself something that you once loved? If you were abused in any way, then you need to make it a top priority to love and nurture yourself. Speaking kindly to yourself is a great way to begin loving the little one within. How often do you have fun the way you used to have fun as a child? When was the last time you allowed yourself to laugh so much that your stomach hurt?

When that little child within is still wounded, this will impact how you feel about yourself, how you act, what choices you make, and how you live your life. I often hear my patients say, "I cannot believe how hurt or angry I am about that situation." Again, whenever you are faced with a situation that elicits stronger feelings than the situation is likely to warrant, most likely this is tapping into some old repressed emotions. If your childhood was difficult, then it is likely that you stuffed some of your feelings. These feelings MUST come out at some point, or you will act them out by making poor choices and doing things that stop you from having your heart's desires.

Over the years, many individuals I counseled stated that they still felt like a child on the inside because they never grew up. This was due to their unhealed childhood issues. As they began to heal, and take great care of themselves, they started to grow back up and became the adults they were meant to be.

Taking care of yourself takes work, especially if you were never properly cared for as a child. You may resent the fact that you now have to be a great parent to yourself, since you did not get what you needed in childhood. It is fine if you feel some temporary resentment. However, if you did not get the good stuff when you were growing up, then you will need to provide it to yourself now. Do not wait for that perfect person or expect your partner to fulfill all your needs. This is not your partner's job. People can help, but the majority of the work needs to come from you. You will exhaust others if you expect them to meet all your needs. That is not other people's job. This is your job.

The rewards that come from growing yourself back up are going to be worth all your efforts. You will no longer have a parent/child relationship with your significant other, you will feel great about yourself, and you will be free to make choices that significantly add to your life. Staying stuck in anger that you did not get what you needed during childhood will only hold you back. You have a right to be angry about this, but you need to work through that anger. Make a commitment today to be a wonderful parent to yourself! Once you get in the habit of doing this, your self-love will flourish.

As you heal, it is a MUST for you to comfort yourself as much as possible. One of the fastest ways to be comforted is by doing what I call the five-minute hug meditation. You may want to record the meditations that are mentioned throughout this book, so that you can easily do them. You can also purchase one of my meditation CDs by visiting my Web site www.normalight.com. Give this meditation a try and see how much better you feel afterwards.

Five-Minute Hug Meditation

To begin, gently close your eyes and slowly take three deep breaths in through your nose and out through your mouth. With every breath you take, you are becoming more relaxed. You are now walking in nature. A gentle breeze is caressing your skin. You feel peaceful. As you continue to walk in this beautiful place, you notice that there are many people sitting around a garden that has a water fountain in the middle. You cannot make out who they are, but you feel drawn to walk toward them. As you walk closer, you see that everyone who has ever loved you is gathered around this peaceful place. They are all waiting to hug and support you. As you slowly hug each person, you feel so much love and comfort. Tears are rolling down your cheeks as you fully realize how truly loved you are. Take in as much love and comfort as you need. Now that you have received all the love and comfort you need, you are going to slowly come back in the room. Take a deep breath in through your nose and out through your mouth. Feel your feet on the floor and open your eyes.

Be kind to yourself. Do this meditation often. By doing this technique whenever you experience any upset or stress, you will be giving yourself the gift of comfort and peace. This meditation will also help you to be in a good state. Do not worry whether you are doing this exactly right. If you feel more peaceful than you did before you did this exercise, then it is working.

Now that you are on your new journey toward becoming healed, get in the habit of comforting yourself automatically. Most people are unaware of how they can do this. Besides meditating, perhaps you can comfort yourself by snuggling up with your favorite blanket and reading a good book. Relaxing on your favorite chair may bring you comfort. Taking a warm bath with scented candles may do the trick. Listening to inspirational music can powerfully comfort you. Take a few minutes to focus on five ways that you can comfort yourself. Look at this list often until you automatically do these things daily. Keep adding to your list. Even if you do not feel like comforting yourself, JUST DO IT!

The five ways that I can comfort myself are by:

1. _____
2. _____
3. _____
4. _____
5. _____

Amanda had a miscarriage only months before her husband died. For a couple of months after these two great losses, Amanda felt as though her whole world had been permanently shattered. Amanda's family and friends tried to help her as much as possible. In spite of all the help she received, she still felt all alone. Deep in her heart, Amanda knew that no one could fully understand how her losses impacted her.

After Amanda and I worked together for a while, she made a commitment to completely work on healing her whole life. Amanda told me that she not only wanted to heal from losing her husband and child, but that she also wanted to heal unresolved childhood issues that always seemed to get in the way of her being fully happy. Talk about being brave! Amanda also mentioned that she was willing to do whatever it took to create a great life. She certainly was determined! Her determination paid off. Amanda not only worked on healing through two incredible losses, but she also worked on being free from the past.

Amanda is now living a great life! Throughout the course of our work together, she got remarried. Amanda said that not only is she happy with her new husband but she is also grateful for her stepchildren. Amanda said, "I finally feel peaceful, happy, and good enough. From going through everything that I went through, this helped me to become more compassionate, caring, and loving." It also helped her to be courageous enough to fully heal from the past. Amanda is stronger and more confident than ever! There were many times when Amanda doubted that she would ever have a good life again after her losses. However, she just kept feeling, healing, and taking one day at a time. Amanda's healing and progress did not happen overnight. There were many times throughout our work together when Amanda tried to convince me that she was worthless and not good enough and that she would never be healed. Even though Amanda still experiences occasional sadness, this no longer consumes her. If you met Amanda today, she would tell you to take one step at a time on your healing journey and that if she could do it, then so can you!

Your past will hold you back until you move through feelings that are stopping you from living a beautiful life in the present. By putting the past behind you, you will no longer be blocking your future possibilities; however, you must heal before you can freely move forward. When you are carrying around old wounds, you walk around as though you are half alive. Your mind will be full of racing thoughts and your feelings will weigh you down. In order to be on the road toward peace and happiness, you will need to heal.

If you have ever been exposed to any form of abuse during your childhood, whether emotional, verbal, physical, or sexual, then you were automatically handed by people and situations a small box filled with bad feelings and lies about yourself and life. Within that box are small cassettes filled with negative, defeating messages that you automatically play over and over in your mind. Even if you have not been abused, you may have acquired that ugly box. When you are feeling physically unwell, stressed, overwhelmed, or vulnerable, your tapes will automatically play in your mind. As you listen to those tapes, you cannot help but feel bad about yourself and life. Your small box of lies will remain a part of your life; this can be very debilitating until you get rid of it.

You can destroy that box! The way to shrink that ugly box of lies is by being loving and kind to yourself with your thoughts, words, and actions. When you feel unworthy, tell yourself that you are more than worthy. Positive, loving people can also help you to shrink your box. They will see the good in you, and this will help you see the good in yourself. The more good you see in yourself, the easier it will be to change your thinking. If you are struggling with feeling good about yourself, keep working at reprogramming your mind with loving, kind thoughts toward yourself. Before you know it, you will have permanently destroyed more lies.

Every time you say something loving and kind to yourself, not only are you working toward destroying the box of lies but you are recording over those tapes. There is great power in creating new tapes that are filled with positive messages that you can listen to throughout your day. You may struggle with this for a while. Keep struggling until you master self-love. You cannot be peaceful and happy, no matter how great your life is, if you do not like or love yourself. When you love who you are, you will no longer tolerate anything that is negative and that does not add to your life. Even if you had great parents or a good childhood, truly loving yourself takes work. You can have great parents and still carry old wounds from the past. Ask anyone who was bullied, even if only one time, how much that experience impacted them. Being bullied can be traumatic. Children who are bullied tell themselves that something is wrong with them. Wham, they now have a box of lies that they will need to get rid of.

I have counseled people from all walks of life who felt and believed that they were worthless. I was not buying into that lie. I will also not buy into the lie that you are worthless! This can become debilitating and hold you back in life. Perhaps you are in the ugly habit of continuing to tell yourself lies. In order to get rid of the belief and feeling that you are worthless, you not only need to eliminate the lies, but you need to do some internal work. Along with feeling, and changing your thinking, you need to believe that you are worthy.

When life hits you hard, it is very difficult to see the truth about yourself and your inner light will be temporarily covered by a variety of feelings. When you are peaceful and happy, your inner light will shine! Therefore, the essence of who you are will powerfully impact everyone around you.

"Nothing can dim the light which shines from within."
— *Maya Angelou*

Nothing can dim your inner light; however, unfelt feelings will temporarily coat it. Think of a lightbulb that shines brightly when nothing is in its way. If you put mud on this bulb, it will still be brilliant, but you will not able to see or experience the illumination. The same is true for you. Your inner light is shining, but you need to get rid of the mud that unfelt feelings create within. Once you get rid of the mud, your inner light is going to glow! As your inner light shines brightly, you can enter a situation where darkness exists and light up the room!

Kim experienced great suffering throughout her life. She was sexually abused as a child. Her husband and mother were verbally and emotionally abusive toward her. Kim is a kind, caring person. Kim said that she feels completely worthless and that she deserves to suffer because she is a terrible person. If you ever met Kim, you would know that this is a total and complete lie. Kim's experiences, as a child and as a wounded adult, have led her down a path of self-hatred.

How are you like Kim? Do you feel worthless because of lies that you were told throughout your life? If you are currently stuck in those lies, you may be thinking right now, "Norma, you do not know me. I am a worthless, horrible person." Wow! You are going to feel so much lighter and freer when you get rid of your negative thinking. You can reverse the impact of your self-abusive behavior right now. The way to do this is to stop putting yourself down in your thoughts and words. Tell yourself that you are completely worthy. It does not matter that you currently do not believe this. Just keep feeding yourself this message and in time you will believe and experience this truth. The human spirit is very powerful. It is more than possible to go from feeling negative feelings toward yourself to becoming healed and seeing that you are more than worthy!

Lauren also experienced much suffering from losing her father, and from her divorce after thirty-two years of marriage. When Lauren was in the midst of her terrible pain, she knew that her faith would get her through all the difficulties that she faced and that "Everything happens for a reason." Her faith, inner strength, and courage helped her to work through her losses.

Lauren is now one of the most positive, optimistic people that you could possibly meet! She has an incredible ability to touch people's lives. Her inner light shines so brightly that you cannot help but be positively impacted by simply being in her presence. People often tell Lauren that she is an amazing inspiration for not letting her traumas and losses destroy her life. Instead, she enjoys each and every day to the fullest. If she did not develop her spirituality, heal her pain, take great care of herself, remain positive, feel great about herself, and be a very giving person, then no one would recognize her inner light. The thick mud would do a good job of concealing it.

Lauren knows that there is nothing but good things in store for her. This is a woman who has been able to pick herself up from the rubble, soar in life, and shine. Her inner light is the same as yours; however, she took all of the necessary steps so that her light could shine powerfully! People love to be around her because they feel great being in her presence. You cannot help but feel great when you are either immersed in your own inner glow or around someone else's.

"Every person has a purpose and a reason for being on earth."
— *Sanaya Roman*

You are not alone with being handed a box of lies about yourself. Most people have a box of lies about who they are and what they are capable of. These lies become the reference point in later life that people turn to when making decisions. HOW SAD! During my childhood, I believed that I was not smart, had no talents, and that I could not do anything right. I never thought that I could possibly amount to anything. When I was seventeen, I thought that college was certainly out of the question for me, but it was not.

I was convinced very early in life that I was not college material since I believed that I was not smart or capable. To this day, it saddens me to think back to one particular day that stands out in my mind. I remember walking on a sidewalk as I was heading back to my apartment at the age of nineteen. I told myself at that moment that just maybe somehow, some way, I would be able to earn an Associate's degree, so that I could become a hotel manager. At that time, I had been working at a restaurant as a waitress and I completely dreaded going to work. I was also taking a few classes at a local community college. I purposely registered for the easiest classes I could take. I just kept praying and hoping that I would be able to pass all the required classes so that I could become a hotel manager. I figured that if I became a hotel manager, then there was some possibility of not dreading what I was doing for a living.

After I took college classes for one year, I discovered that I was a good college student. In my second year of college, I learned that not only was I capable but I could excel in all my classes! After I discovered how capable I was and my confidence grew, I changed my major. I realized that my heart was truly set on helping people. Once I matriculated my credits to a four-year college, I was notified by the university that since my grades were so good, I could apply for a scholarship! The moment I discovered that I got the scholarship, I was blissful! To think that only a few years earlier I thought that I was not capable of being a college student and now I was the recipient of a scholarship. That was incredible!

My final pivotal moment that impacted me was when I got accepted into a very competitive Ph.D. program. During my eight-hour interview,

I was in awe of some of my competitors. All the candidates on that interview were very accomplished. A month after my interview, I held my acceptance letter in my hand. The moment I read my acceptance letter was the moment that I realized for the first time in my life that anything is truly possible!

If I continued to hold on to the lie that I was not smart, then I never would be where I am today. Let go of your debilitating lies. Take a few minutes to think about the lies that you were given throughout your life.

Some of the lies that I was given about myself are:

_____

_____

_____

_____

How have these lies impacted you? These lies have impacted me by:

_____

_____

_____

_____

How would your life be different if you no longer believed any of these lies? If I no longer believed those lies, then:

_____

_____

_____

_____

The lies that you are holding on to are not only debilitating, but they can be damaging. Some of those lies have the power to hold you back in life. Have you ever felt a great desire to do something, but you stop yourself? Perhaps some lies about your intelligence or what you are capable of are holding you back from pursuing what you want. You may tell yourself that you are not intelligent or capable enough, so why bother? Two of the most common lies I see are that people believe they are worthless and not good enough. These lies will create pain and doubt in anyone. People often mask the pain that those lies cause through some form of addiction. I have never met anyone who did not have a box of lies at some point in their life! Some people may have a box of lies the size of a ring box, while others have a box that can fill a room.

There are millions of children on earth who believe that they are no good and worthless. These little children will then grow up to be wounded adults who will act out their lies. People who make poor choices in life are certainly not able to see the truth about themselves. It took many years of healing and spiritual growth for me to no longer accept others' lies about who I am. Now that you are ready to free yourself, let this meditation help you to get started with getting rid of the lies.

Net Meditation

Slowly take a deep breath in through your nose and out through your mouth. Do this three times. When you are ready, gently close your eyes and walk on the beach. You have a big net in your hand that has the power to absorb all the lies that you were given throughout your life. Were you told that you are incompetent, useless, or not good enough? Put those lies in your net. Keep filling up your net with all the lies that you were given or that you gave yourself. Once all your lies are in the net, throw them, with great force, in the ocean. They are now being completely destroyed as you look at that big explosion. The fumes from the explosion make you feel great joy by knowing that you are free.

Become fully aware of how good it feels to get rid of the heavy burden of carrying around those lies. You are now running on the beach; you feel great joy and happiness from your new freedom. The warmth from the sun and sand also help you feel good. Slowly take a deep breath in through your nose and out through your mouth. Walk back on the sand and sit on the bench that is in front of you. A bright white light is shining all around you. You feel very peaceful at this moment. Stay focused on how good you feel.

When you are ready, ask your intuition to tell you three truths about yourself. Listen carefully to your intuition. If your information is not positive, get that net again and destroy your lies until you hear your intuition speak lovingly to you. The information that you receive will be nothing but positive and good. Once you are done hearing three truths about yourself, see the light shining even brighter on the top of your head and in your heart.

Now bring this light in the room. It is completely surrounding your body where you are sitting. Before you open your eyes, take a deep breath *in through your nose and out through your mouth. Open your eyes and come back in the room.* Hold on to these good feelings as long as you can. What truths did you receive about yourself? Take a few minutes to write about these truths.

The truths that I received about myself were:

_____

_____

_____

_____

_____

Where are you going to post these truths, so that you can see them every day? The more you focus on your truths, the easier it will be to continue to destroy the lies. How did it feel to get rid of those lies? What was it like to hear those truths about yourself? Do not worry if you have trouble receiving information. It is okay! Just keep at this until you do. Most people will have trouble getting to their truth because they have many layers of lies that they need to get rid of first. Once you get to your truths, hold on to them and continue to focus on these truths as they become your anchor in life! Your new truths will help you to create freedom in your life!

When you are in emotional pain, unable to see a spark of light, this will leave you guessing where life is taking you. At that point, you may have trouble believing that you can live a life of total freedom, but you can. Which areas of your life are in need of freedom? Are you in need of this from inner turmoil, worry, anxiety, depression, doubt, confusion, people-pleasing, making poor choices, or settling for mediocrity? Do you need freedom from dissatisfying relationships? Have you been longing to be free from that extra weight? Are you ready to get rid of that debt? Once you are healed and in your power, you will be well on your way to creating these freedoms for yourself!

Great things often come from pain and suffering. One good thing is that when your life is better than ever, you will not take this for granted; you will relish and fully appreciate your life. The challenge lies in getting through the temporary healing. You may feel as though you will never move beyond your current situation and have total freedom. You will! The key is to persevere and move forward, one step at a time, with faith. I know that it is challenging to move forward when you are experiencing uncomfortable emotions, but keep doing it anyway.

"Life is a personal mission. You have a calling that exists only for you and that only you can fulfill."
— *Naomi Stephan, Ph.D.*

The most inspirational people tend to be the ones who have gone through some of the worst traumas and losses. The only difference between you and them is that you are where they used to be. Regardless of where you are in your healing process, you need to believe that you are meant to have total freedom in every area of your life. Once you are emotionally free, you will see how truly magnificent you are and what you have to offer this world.

PART II

Creating Inner Peace

CHAPTER 3

How to De-Stress Your Life

We all experience stress to one degree or another. However, too much stress will negatively impact your body, mind, and spirit. It will stop you from experiencing peace and joy. People often ignore stress in their lives, until they experience major health issues. Does that sound like you? Do you ignore your stress so that you can move forward with your to-do list? This is a problem. Daily de-stressing is the solution. It will not only make you feel better, but will decrease your chances of developing health problems.

My patients who have de-stressed daily as they healed were able to move through the healing process with more ease and grace than some of my patients who did not make this a daily practice. Having uncomfortable feelings and a difficult situation to move through is VERY STRESSFUL. I have counseled some people who were under tremendous stress and were not even aware of it until I pointed it out to them. Their constant health issues were a big clue. As you heal, it is a must to de-stress daily. Make this one of your top priorities. This will help you on your journey!

Just today, I felt much stress from having to finish some writing projects. In order for me to accomplish this goal, I had to work more hours than usual. By late afternoon, my stress increased so much that I was feeling unhappy. At that point, I realized that I needed to drop everything for twenty minutes and de-stress, which I often do by meditating. After I meditated, the stress was completely gone. I felt refreshed and peaceful, which helped me to easily accomplish what I had set out to do.

Some of the most energetic and beautiful people on earth are the ones who consistently eat well, exercise, meditate, and nurture themselves. These things help to decrease stress significantly and keep you looking and feeling your best. When was the last time you ate well, exercised, meditated, and nurtured yourself all in one day? The key to making de-stressing a daily part of your life is to make it a top priority. Is this currently a top priority of yours? If not, it needs to be. When was the last time you nurtured yourself and were able to de-stress? How do you nurture yourself?

Have you ever thought about taking "a me day" off from work? You may have told yourself that you cannot do this. Yes, you can! Now you have something to look forward to. The more you nurture yourself in ways that add to your life, the more you will de-stress. As you heal, nurture yourself as much as possible. You will greatly benefit from this!

If money is a concern, keep in mind that there are many creative ways to nurture yourself without spending much money. Why not take some treats to your favorite place in nature and enjoy the beauty that this environment has to offer? Listening to music that energizes your spirit is a great way to nurture yourself. When was the last time you did a crazy and wild dance in front of your mirror when no one was looking? Laugh at how silly you can be when you dance freely. By being good to yourself, you are also modeling to others how they can be good to themselves.

It is imperative to have "me time." When was the last time you put yourself on the calendar? When was the last time you pampered yourself for a couple of hours? You may be thinking that you have too many things to do to spare time for this. This is one of the reasons you may have a lot of stress in your life. Get rid of that thought. Instead, make yourself a priority throughout your busy day.

There are plenty of things that you can do in fifteen minutes that will make you feel great. On the days when my schedule is completely full, I take those fifteen minutes and savor them as though I am eating my favorite dark chocolate. I find that when I meditate, rest, listen to music, take a walk, talk to a loved one, pray, read, or write for fifteen minutes, it refuels my spirit. There will be days when simply focusing on yourself for fifteen minutes will do the trick to keep you in a good state.

I cannot live without eating well, exercising, meditating, listening to music, and spending time in nature. These things help me instantly feel good and they decrease my stress. How do you instantly feel good? Have you discovered how exercising can powerfully help you to de-stress in a short period of time? Do you exercise regularly? This is a great way to take all the stress you have accumulated and throw it out the door. How about music? If you love music, simply listening to your favorite songs will help you feel good. Add some dancing in front of the mirror for twenty minutes and say good-bye to even more stress.

Once you discover what helps you, get in the habit of doing those things regularly. What excuses did you make in the past for not making de-stressing a daily part of your life? Figure out what they were so you can drop them. Once you get in the habit of de-stressing daily, you will feel better than ever!

"The beginning of a habit is like an invisible thread, but every time we repeat the act we strengthen the strand, add to it another filament, until it becomes a great cable and binds us irrevocably, thought and act."
— *Orison Swett Marden*

The ten ways that I can de-stress regularly are by:

1. _____   6. _____
2. _____   7. _____
3. _____   8. _____
4. _____   9. _____
5. _____   10. _____

Create an Environment That Helps You De-stress

No matter where you live, the place you call "home" needs to help you de-stress. You need to be able to take off your shoes and instantly relax! Does your living space help you do this? If not, what changes do you need to make in order to create a relaxing atmosphere? Is your environment cluttered and messy? If so, this will only create more stress. It does not have to cost you much money to create an environment that feels good and nurturing to your spirit. However, it may take some creativity on your part.

Marissa was a struggling single mother of two living in a dangerous area. The sound of gunshots ringing out was something they grew accustomed to. Marissa couldn't do anything about the violence surrounding their apartment building, but she knew she could create a sanctuary for her little family inside their home. She painted the walls in warm, soothing colors. She saved old glass jars and filled them with translucent colored beads, which she displayed in every room. She arranged vases of beautiful silk flowers around the apartment, and every evening she lit candles whose soothing vanilla scent filled the air. She and her children always kept things neatly in order. You couldn't help but feel relaxed and peaceful inside that apartment, though the harsh reality of the neighborhood was all too real once you stepped outside. It cost Marissa very little money to create a sanctuary that did an enormous amount to help her and her children de-stress in an environment that did its best to keep them on edge.

Do you love your living space? Do you like everything that you own? If you no longer like some of your belongings, then why not donate them to a local charity? Keep in mind that someone else will benefit from what no longer suits you. Go throughout your place and ask yourself, "Do I really like this?" If the answer is "No," then put it in the donation box. You will feel good giving your stuff away, so someone else can appreciate it, rather than fill up space with things that do not add to your life. It can be very cathartic to get rid of things that no longer suit you. This is especially good to do while you are healing. Symbolically, you are reminding yourself that you are on a new path in life where you can have everything that makes you feel good, but first you need to get rid of the old, so that you can make room for the new.

After you donate everything, you will have more room to create an environment that uplifts your spirits and helps you to de-stress. You will then be able to fill up the empty space with the exact things you love. Once you create an environment that nurtures you, all you have to do is quiet your mind, relax, and let your environment take your stress away. Voilà Enjoy!

Meditating

The one thing you can always count on to help you to de-stress in less than ten minutes is meditation. Once you do this regularly, the benefits will be so great that you will realize you cannot live without it. Meditating will also help you to become centered and change your state of mind very quickly. Give the meditations in chapter 5 a try and enjoy the peace that you will feel after doing them!

Ways to De-Stress

One way to keep your stress very low is by checking in with yourself. Each day, examine how much stress you have by using a scale in your mind from 1 to 10. The goal is to keep your stress as low as possible. Whenever you reach 3 or more, it is time to do something to de-stress. This scale helps me. It brings my attention to the fact that I am experiencing a certain degree of stress and that I need to take action in order to decrease it. It will help you, too. Once you get in the habit of checking in with yourself and de-stressing, you will be more peaceful than ever! Your body, mind, and spirit will thank you for doing this.

Another great way to de-stress is by feeding your inner spirit. Your inner spirit needs to be fed daily, just as you need to eat daily. Most people will spiritually starve themselves and wonder why they have no energy and motivation; they drag themselves through life on empty. They may even snap at others due to their spiritual starvation. You have witnessed this behavior. When you were standing on line, waiting to pay for your groceries, you might have heard the person in front of you snap at the cashier. At that moment, what you are witnessing is a person who was in great need of spiritual nourishment. Someone who is well nourished is not going to snap at a cashier, but politely be assertive. When you are not feeling peaceful or you are irritated, this means that you have neglected to feed yourself. As you heal, it is a must to feed your spirit several times a day. Once you get in the habit of doing this, your attitude, state, and energy level will improve. You will feel more peaceful and relaxed.

Nature is a great way to feed yourself that requires very little effort on your part. All you need to do is appreciate the beauty around you and you will be fed. Many of my patients who have gone through horrific losses mentioned that this was one of the few things that comforted them as they healed. I enjoy feeding myself in this way, too. When I am running on the beach or at the reservoir, I cannot help but feel great as I appreciate all the beauty around me. When has nature fed your spirit? Where were you? What were you doing? When is the next time you plan on letting nature feed you?

Giving to others is another great way to nourish yourself. Giving from the heart and feeding your spirit does not have to cost a cent. Your spirit will ALWAYS be fed when you give from the heart. People who are not very giving do not even realize that they are actually depriving themselves from great nourishment. Nothing but joy comes when you give from the heart.

Reading or listening to something that inspires you will surely feed your spirit. How about listening to inspirational music as you head off to work in the morning? How often do you start your day by reading inspirational quotes? Even though feeding your spirit and nurturing yourself go hand in hand, feeding your spirit requires something more powerful, since it directly impacts your heart. How do you feed yourself on a daily basis? Take a few minutes to honestly answer this question.

> *"How beautiful it is to do nothing,*
> *and then to rest afterward."*
> *— Spanish Proverb*

Whenever you feel peaceful, by feeding your spirit, your state will begin to change. With just the right amount of spiritual food, you will feel great. When you are carrying a heavy emotional backpack, feeding your spirit will temporarily help you put that backpack on the ground, while you rest. Once you eat your spiritual meal, you will have more energy and strength to walk through your healing.

As you work toward living your best life, it is a must to feed your spirit regularly. On some days, you will need to do this for twenty minutes and on other days you may need to feed it for a couple of hours. What have you read that feeds your spirit? Why not take some of those words and write them on paper where you can read them as you look in the mirror? Perhaps this thought never occurred to you. There is great power in reading things that uplift you. What do you secretly wish that others would do for you? Good, now you have something that you can do for yourself. Notice how you feel every time you do something that feeds your spirit. If you do not have much time on certain days, then do a quick meditation for ten minutes. Here is a meditation that can powerfully help you on those very busy days.

My Ideal Day Meditation

To begin, take a deep breath in and relax. You are now waking up in the most peaceful place that you have ever seen, as you begin your ideal day. Look all around you and slowly absorb the magnificence of this place. Your heart feels so much excitement and joy now that you are fully removed from everything. Take in all of the love and joy that this special place has to offer. In front of you is a piece of paper. You are going to make a list of five things that you would love to do on this day. Perhaps you want to take a walk on the beach or go hiking in the woods. Maybe you want to read a book and relax. Now see yourself doing all the things on your list with great pleasure. Your spirit is being completely nourished by the happiness and joy that you are experiencing on this glorious day. Feel the joy even more. When you are ready, slowly come back to the room. Feel your feet on the floor and gently open your eyes. Do this meditation as often as you need.

Sometimes throughout the healing process, you may feel malnourished. Most people feel this way at some point as they heal. If meditating helps you, then do this often until you are full. Throughout my healing, I had to meditate several times a day. This was one of the few things that nourished me. There is nothing wrong with nourishing your spirit. In fact, this needs to be a must all throughout your life.

Another good way to have something to look forward to every day is to eat a delicious meal. This will add an exciting spark to your life. What can you look forward to each day? I enjoy coffee. Everyone who knows me can attest to this truth. Every morning, I look forward to coming down my stairs to the smell of delicious coffee that is brewed a few minutes before I wake up. Even though I only drink two cups of decaffeinated coffee a day, this small pleasure adds joy to my life. Whenever you experience joy, your spirit is being fed. There are countless ways to add things in your life that you can look forward to.

Why not go away for a weekend? How about saving for your dream vacation? This will give you something to look forward to. Having things to look forward to will reinforce that life can be good and exciting. The more you focus on the positive things about your life, the more you will attract the same and be open to unlimited possibilities. This will open up a whole new world of joy and happiness for you, which will make your spirit dance.

Having fun offers great nourishment and is a great way to de-stress. While you are healing, you may only experience small doses of this. As you move through the healing process, it will become a bigger part of your life. When was the last time you had fun? How can you experience more of this? Life is not meant to be serious all the time. We are meant to have fun and fully enjoy life. Most people forget to make this a part of their lives. How did you have fun as a child? How did you play? What made you laugh?

When you are ready, make it a point to have fun on a regular basis. One of my favorite ways of doing this is by taking an entire day off from everything and exploring a new town, with a loved one. On those special days, I will eat foods that I typically do not eat and I will buy myself or someone I care about a little something special. I cannot tell you how great I feel when I do this. Do you enjoy listening to live music? If so, go to a live concert. Do you like sports? Treat yourself to a live game. Make a list of five ways that you can have fun and do these things on your list.

"People rarely succeed unless they have fun in what they are doing."
— Dale Carnegie

I can have fun by:

1. _____
2. _____
3. _____
4. _____
5. _____

Doing these things on your list will help to clear your mind from daily pressures and stress. It will also put you in a good state and help you as you heal. Yes, you can give yourself breaks from your feelings as you move through your healing. In fact, this is necessary. The next time you do one of the things on your list, become aware of how great you feel, so that you can create more of this. What we focus on expands, and when we focus on the positives, we experience positive emotions.

When was the last time you allowed yourself to be creative in your mind? Take a few minutes to imagine yourself doing the most outrageous things that make you laugh. This will quickly change your state of mind. If you visualize yourself having lots of fun, then your body will reap the rewards by making you feel more relaxed and at ease. Spend time each week with people who make you laugh. This will quickly feed your spirit. Find humor in as many things as possible. It is important not to take life so seriously all the time. Who and what makes you laugh? How can you add more of this in your life? When was the last time you laughed at yourself? We all do and say silly things from time to time.

I laugh at myself often. I seem to have many funny, silly things happen to me. A few years ago, I experienced one at the gym when I saw the most handsome man I had ever seen. As soon as I came directly in contact with him, I tripped over the leg press machine and practically fell on the floor. After I pulled my hands off the floor, which saved me from completely falling on my face, my iPod and headphones went flying in the air. I casually picked up my iPod. Then my water bottle slid out of my hand and spilled water onto the carpet. The gentleman probably thought I was an idiot. I felt embarrassed. My breathing came to a halt for a few seconds. However, I just picked up my water bottle and walked away. As I was walking away, I could not help but laugh at myself. The whole situation was very funny. Laugh at yourself. This can be so much fun! You do not need to apologize for taking good care of yourself. As you grow and evolve, be flexible with discovering even more ways that you can feed your spirit.

In order to fully feed your inner spirit, you must first take good care of your body and mind. Some people may focus on their mind and spirit, yet neglect their bodies. It is easy to neglect your body while going through the hustle and bustle of everyday life. If you're like most people, you have a very busy schedule and you may use that as your excuse for not exercising regularly and eating well. There should be no excuses for not eating well and exercising regularly. Your emotional, mental, and physical health are directly affected by these two factors. Perhaps being out of shape and overweight is one more thing that you can beat yourself up over.

Some people naturally love to exercise, while others cringe at the thought. If you dread thinking about exercising, then you have not discovered an exercise regimen that works for you. When you were younger, what type of exercise did you enjoy? Did you enjoy riding your bike? How about walking or running? Were you actively involved in sports? Did you enjoy dancing? Add those things back in your life. Once you talk to your doctor about finding an exercise and eating program that works best for you, slowly change your eating and exercise routine. When starting an exercise program, do not set yourself up for failure by pushing yourself too much. This is a big mistake that most people make. You will only get frustrated and talk yourself out of exercising. It will not work. Start off slowly, then gradually increase the amount of time you work out. Be proud of yourself for making the commitment to exercise!

When you get in the habit of exercising on a regular basis, you are going to feel much better about yourself and your life. Exercising has the power to make you feel good not only physically but mentally. Exercising will automatically change your state of mind and help you to de-stress. Think of a time when you were feeling down and you decided to go for a walk. By the time you finished your walk, you no doubt felt much better. Exercising offers positive results! Too many people focus on how much they hate exercising. Remember, what we tell ourselves will create our feelings. If you say you "hate" anything, then this will conjure up negative feelings and you will resist doing what you "hate." As you hold on to your resistance, exercising will become even more difficult. If you change your thinking about exercising, then you no longer have to dread your workouts. Stay focused on how great you will feel after your workout. Why not reward yourself one time a month for working out regularly? This will surely motivate you! Stay positive and make exercising your new healthy habit.

When I am feeling much stress or having a bad day, all I have to do is go to the gym for one hour and my state will completely change. I often change my workout routine based on how I am feeling. When I am feeling overwhelmed, I will run on the treadmill, as I listen to my iPod. Running and listening to music helps me to get back to feeling great. If I have much on my mind, I will take a spinning cycle class. I discovered that spinning helps me to fully clear my mind. If I am feeling stress in my body, all I have to do is lift weights, and within one hour, my body feels great. Keep experimenting until you find a workout program that works best for you and one that you do not dread. Be kind to yourself before, during, and after your workout. Do not tell yourself, "Gee, I am a fat slob, so why even work out? I should just forget about exercising since I hate it in the first place." How about saying, "I am proud of myself for exercising today. If I keep at this long enough, then I will feel and look better." Just because your body is not at your ideal weight does not mean you should make things worse by being mean to yourself with your thoughts, actions, and words.

Some people who avoid feelings may medicate themselves with food. This may temporarily comfort you, but now you are creating more unhappiness and stress by being out of shape and overweight. Plus, whatever emotions you stuff with food are still inside you. Why not feel and work out at the same time? This will be a win-win situation. After you work out, your state will be good. You will work toward losing that weight and feel much better. Plus, you will not have to revisit those emotions at a later date. They will already be released because you will have felt them. When you stuff yourself with unhealthy foods, how can you possibly feel good when you literally feel sick to your stomach? You cannot. Stop trying to find a quick fix for your weight problem. Quick fixes do not work.

Eating well and exercising will not only help you feel better, but will give you more energy, help you think more clearly, and help you reach your optimum health. The better you take care of your body, the better your body will take care of you! Now that you are working on taking great care of yourself, it is important to design an eating and exercise plan that you can live with for the rest of your life, where you feel good and energized. If you eat very healthily, then you can say good-bye to your unhealthy cravings. This may be hard to believe, but it is true! Eating well and exercising are essential for you to feel and look your very best!

If I did not eat well, I would be dragging my feet each day. Eating well not only helps me feel great, but it gives me lots of energy. I have had friends tell me that they are amazed by how much energy I have. This is simply because of my healthy eating and exercise habits. I was fortunate at a young age to get in the habit of eating well and exercising regularly. You, too, can make this a good habit of yours, starting today! Experiment with discovering which foods make your body feel good and which foods make you feel lousy. If your stomach is upset from eating something, then make a mental note of this. If you feel sluggish and tired after you eat, then your body is letting you know that what you just ate is not working for you. The more you begin to love your body, the more you will be in tune with what your body needs. There is no magic formula to eating well. Everyone's body is different. Find what works best for you!

Sue beat herself up for years for being overweight. She tried many diets that did not work. Once she started feeling emotions she had stuffed, her weight began to automatically drop. Sue said to me, "You were right, now that I am feeling my feelings, my weight is starting to melt away." She was amazed to discover that since she was no longer comforting herself with food, her weight had no choice but to come off. What Sue experienced is quite common. Many of my patients have lost much weight based on simply feeling, rather than medicating themselves with food. When you feel, this is an act of self-love. When you love who you are, you will automatically want to eat better and you will comfort yourself in healthy ways, rather than stuffing yourself to a state of numbness. By eating well, exercising, and comforting yourself in healthy ways, you will have to say good-bye to your extra weight.

Most women in our society are very unhappy with their bodies. The media is constantly bombarding women and girls with messages that say you need to look youthful and be very thin, which make women and girls feel worthless and stressful when they cannot live up to this standard. Every week, at least one of my female patients will tell me how worthless she feels because her body is not perfect. I know that it can be very challenging to accept your body when you are uncomfortable in your own skin. However, this is completely necessary. The way to begin accepting your body is by being kind toward your body with your thoughts, actions, and words. As you consistently eat well and exercise, it will be easier for you to accept your body. Acceptance needs to begin at this very moment, regardless of how you look.

You can begin by saying to yourself, "Now that I am taking care of my body, I am feeling and looking better every day." Even if you are very unhappy with your weight, wear things that make you look and feel good. If you are unhappy with yourself when you are heavy, then you will be unhappy with yourself when you lose that weight. The more you accept yourself today, the more you will make a lifetime commitment to eat well and to exercise. When speaking to someone, do not put yourself down because you do not like your body. Take action each day toward accepting and loving your body. No negative thoughts! These thoughts only create stress.

I have witnessed people simply change one thing in their diet, and the impact from that one change was profound. Sally told me that she could not understand why her five-year-old son had so much trouble falling asleep after she put him to bed. She felt much stress every night from her son not being able to sleep. When I counseled Sally for the first time, she told me that he had trouble falling asleep for over three months. His doctor and other professionals could not figure out why he had trouble falling asleep. He was having trouble staying awake during school. He also cried easily and was very irritated.

Whenever someone has trouble falling asleep, the first question I ask is whether they are eating or drinking anything within a few hours of bedtime that contains caffeine. Often that is the case. When I asked Sally whether she gave her son anything to drink or eat after 5:00 that contained caffeine, she said, "No." Then I asked her if she ever gave her son hot chocolate before bed. She said, "Yes, every night." That was the culprit! The hot chocolate she was giving him contained caffeine. She cut out the nightly drink and his sleeping problems disappeared.

Taking good care of the body also means resting when your body is in need of rest. How often do you rest when this is clearly what your body needs? Many people keep themselves busy as a way of running away from their feelings. This can create stress and health problems. It is a must to be a responsible individual and do what needs to be done; however, resting is very important and a great way to de-stress. If you do not get the proper amount of rest, you cannot be in a good state of mind and you will not be taking good care of your body. I have discovered that when I am exhausted, my thoughts and feelings become negative. When I found myself in a negative state last year for no reason, I was baffled. Soon it became clear that I was exhausted simply from being too busy.

Once I discovered what was happening, I made it a priority to rest. After I rested, my state quickly returned to where I felt happy and peaceful. Keep checking in with yourself. If you discover that you are suddenly in a bad state for no apparent reason, it may be that you simply need to rest.

Keep in tune with your body. Whenever a patient of mine tells me that they feel agitated and upset, but they do not know why, the first question I ask is if they feel exhausted. In every case, the answer was "yes." The next time you are agitated and upset, discover if you simply need to rest. Your body is constantly speaking to you. It is important to take the time to listen. Once you discover what your body needs, stop making excuses for not taking care of yourself and meeting those needs!

Controlled breathing is another great way to take care of your body and decrease stress. By doing controlled breathing for five minutes a day, not only will you immediately feel better, but your body will continue to benefit from the results throughout the day. Here is a simple breathing technique you can do every morning after you wake up and whenever you are experiencing stress or tension.

Controlled Breathing Technique

Lie or sit in a comfortable place. Cross one hand directly on top of the other. Place them on your stomach, just below your navel. Take a slow deep breath in through your nose, see your stomach expand like a balloon. Now slowly exhale through your mouth until all the air is gone. Do this two more times. Now place your hands on your diaphragm, which is that hollow place in the center just below your ribs. You are going to slowly expand that area by breathing in through the nose. Once that area is fully expanded, slowly exhale. Repeat this two more times. The third place that you are going to gently place your hands is over your clavicle. Now that your hands are placed just below your throat, you are going to breathe in through your nose, while fully expanding that area. Then slowly exhale through the mouth. Do this two more times.

When you get in the habit of doing controlled breathing regularly, you will be glad that you did! Make taking care of your body a regular part of your day and get ready for some wonderful benefits!

Support yourself with de-stressing on a daily basis. As you begin to get in this good habit, you will begin to enjoy life more than ever. When you do not have much time, remember that you can powerfully de-stress by doing a meditation or immersing yourself in nature. The more you de-stress, the happier you will be and the better you will feel. You owe it to your mind, body, and spirit to get in the habit of de-stressing.

CHAPTER 4

How to Love Yourself

*"The greatest gift you can give
yourself is a little
bit of your own attention."*
— *Anthony J. D'Angelo*

You may have heard how important it is to love yourself and just chuckled at that thought and went on your way. But self-hatred is a common problem and it will only lead to a life of misery. You may not even realize that you do not like or, even worse, that you hate yourself. Self-hatred, often expressed through mistreating yourself, makes you a victim to life. Loving yourself will set you free. Perhaps you are going through a difficult situation and are now ready to heal so that you can learn how to love yourself and master this once and for all.

Nothing good comes from mistreating yourself. It is uncomfortable being in the presence of someone who does this. Not liking yourself is toxic, not only to you but to everyone with whom you come in contact. When you do not like who you are, you will carry a toxic vial wherever you go. The fumes from this poison will impact you and everyone around you. NO FUMES! If you have been carrying this poison, get rid of it now! If everyone got rid of their nasty vials, then this world would be a much better place. The only way to get rid of it is by loving yourself through your thoughts, words, and actions. You were made to shine, not hide behind hatred, addictions, or any other form of abuse. Whenever you take great care of yourself, you will emanate a natural flow of love and kindness to everyone and you will be more pleasant to be around.

Loving yourself is a key requirement to living a happy life. When you love yourself, you will feel better, make healthy choices, have more energy, experience more positive outcomes, and be more resilient when facing life's challenges. One of the most powerful ways to love yourself is by feeding yourself positive thoughts and messages.

You have something great to offer this world. You need to know that this is true, regardless of that little negative voice that tells you that you are not worthy and that you have nothing to offer. See a Stop sign in your mind every time that little negative voice shows its ugly self. Then fully destroy those negative thoughts by telling yourself the truth.

How would your life be different right now if you truly loved yourself?

_____

_____

_____

_____

What changes would you make if you loved yourself?

_____

_____

_____

_____

What is holding you back from loving yourself?

_____

_____

_____

_____

Nancy's parents were drug addicts. She never felt loved by them, and therefore never learned how to love herself. She purposely got pregnant at seventeen because Al "paid attention" to her. But Al, also a drug addict, was unable to love her. Nancy said that all she ever wanted in life was to be loved. I let her know that she needed to learn how to love herself first so that she could allow healthy people to love her. I helped Nancy work through her misconceptions and her negative beliefs and thoughts from the past so she could change her way of thinking that wasn't serving her. Eventually Nancy was able to leave her abusive marriage of twenty-two years. Today she talks to young women at homeless shelters and churches about how great life can be when you love yourself and do not allow others to mistreat you.

One strong component to self-love includes taking excellent care of yourself. This begins when you treat precious you very well and you feel good as a result of that treatment. Most people fail to do this. They think that this is "selfish." The truth is that when you take care of yourself, you are refueling your spirit so that you can move forward, without being on empty. Ultimately, this will only help you to be a more giving person. This will also help your healing process.

If you were not properly cared for as a child, then this concept is going to feel uncomfortable at first. In fact, it will seem completely foreign to you. When you grow up in a healthy environment, you will have at least one person model to you how you can take care of yourself. You would then become an adult who automatically takes great care of yourself on a regular basis.

You may be thinking right now, "I cannot take great care of myself since I don't have time." Once you fully make a commitment to change your old patterns, you will create the space to do so. You will suddenly find time to do things that add to your life. To begin this lifelong process, why not ask, "What can I do for myself today that would make me feel good?" Then follow through with taking action toward doing those things. On some days, you may prefer doing something nice for someone else, so follow through with that desire. Being kind and loving to others and walking away feeling good is one more way to be good to yourself.

If possible, avoid the things that keep you feeling down. Yes, you need to process your feelings, but you do not need to embrace the things that continue to make you feel lousy. Surround yourself with people and things that make you feel good. What makes you feel good? Does music do this for you? Then buy a new CD that you love. Do you feel good after you get a massage? Why not treat yourself to a massage as often as you can? Make a list of all the things that help you feel good. Keep this list by your bed, review it before you go to sleep, and keep adding new ways that you can be good to yourself. If you are not ready to take action, simply visualize yourself doing the things that you wrote until they come to fruition. Eventually, you will have fun being good to yourself!

It Is Time to Feel Great About Yourself

In order to live a peaceful life, you must feel great about yourself. If you do not like who you are, then you cannot be happy or enjoy the good in your life. You will simply exist in this world, while feeling not good enough, as your inner storm continues. Do you know that no one on earth is more worthy than you? Stop telling yourself lies that block this truth. Once you heal your wounds, you will see how truly incredible you are!

People often make decisions that will compromise their self-esteem. In order to start feeling good about yourself, consider whether a decision will add to your life, or erode some of your self-esteem. All of us have had circumstances where by choosing instant gratification, we put ourselves at risk of negatively impacting our self-esteem. Not all instant gratification will be harmful, but some will. When you are fully committed to healing and loving yourself, you will no longer compromise your values and self-esteem for some quick fix that will negatively impact you.

If you are doing something that you are ashamed of, now is the time to stop that behavior. We all have made decisions we are not proud of; this is called being human. However, people who are healthy will not continue to do things that make them feel lousy. A healed person will do whatever it takes to preserve their good feelings about themselves. They fully understand the importance of liking yourself over choosing instant gratification that is not healthy for them. The healthiest choice you can make is to feel your feelings, rather than medicate them with instant gratification. Feeling great about yourself is a process. It will take time to accomplish this goal if you have been emotionally beating yourself up for years.

As you heal, grow, and evolve you will continue to see more of your good qualities. Keep your thoughts focused on the positives about yourself. It does not matter how long it takes you to do this, just keep at it until this becomes a habit. If someone puts you down and you calmly stand up for yourself, know that you are moving in the right direction. Remember, no one has a right to disrespect you in any way.

People who have low self-esteem are often consumed by fear rather than freedom, and yet they wonder why they are so unhappy. This may simply be a result of their self-esteem being depleted. You have the power within you to begin today to work toward feeling great about precious YOU! It is time to invest in yourself. When you feel good about yourself, you will embrace the fact that there are unlimited possibilities for your life. When you do not feel good about yourself, then you cannot fully be in your power and you throw those possibilities out the door. You will feel more vulnerable and not take great care of yourself.

When I was seventeen, I felt horrible about myself because I was carrying around a box of lies that I acquired in my childhood. I could not figure out how I would ever feel good about myself when I heard so many negative messages. I intuitively felt led one day to ask all the members from a healing group that I had been participating in for two years if they would write something positive about me on a strip of paper. I then carried those strips of paper everywhere I went. While I was working at a restaurant, I vividly remember feeling so terrible about myself and life that I used to look forward to having to go to the bathroom, just so I could read something positive about myself. I read those messages over and over until I started to believe the positive things that people said about me. That was the very beginning of me destroying ugly lies about myself. Once I started to believe that there was something good about me, my life was never the same. I began to make decisions that were empowering and helped me feel good about myself. I now clearly see that there was nothing wrong with me— I just had major healing to do before I could see the good in myself.

There is nothing wrong with you! You just have some healing to do before you can see how magnificent you are. Carrying around lies will only negatively impact your life. The truth will set you free! Holding on to the truths about yourself has positive power. When you feel good about yourself, your whole life will transform in front of your eyes. Great things are created from positive power. You have the option in this very moment to live in truth, rather than continue to hold on to your lies.

When you do not feel good about yourself, you will be afraid of others rejecting you. When you have a good relationship with yourself, you will no longer be afraid of this. When someone rejects you, you will realize that this says something about the other person, not about you. If people really took the time to get to know you, they would see the beauty in you. The problem is that very few people take the time to get to know each other. How many times have you met someone for the first time and they do not ask you one question about yourself? I would guess that the answer is many. If you have been deeply wounded in the past, and did not heal your wounds, you will continue to be afraid.

When you are healed and like yourself, you will become an inspiration to others. People will admire your strength and confidence. Through you, they will know that they too can live a good life. They will realize that they no longer need to follow the crowd and settle for a mediocre life. On some level, most people want to be healed, but they are afraid to do the work that it takes to get there. They intuitively know that this is a warrior's journey. You are that warrior!

Another way to feel good about yourself is by being kind to others even when they are not kind to you. Responding positively to a person who is not kind to you can be very difficult. However, you will feel great about how you handled the situation. Let your intuition guide you with handling all situations powerfully. There may be times when you simply need to walk away from someone who is not kind to you, without saying a word. Follow your intuition because it will powerfully guide you and let you know what to do. People who are intentionally not kind to others do not realize that they are only harming themselves. They have to live with their darkness, not you.

You have a gift for this world that only you can offer. You cannot offer what you are meant to offer if you continue to hurt yourself or others. If you have intentionally hurt others, look at the self that you are creating. It certainly does not feel good to be that way. You can change this way of being NOW! Each of us can make the decision to completely transform our lives at any given moment. Now that you are on the path of creating inner peace, joy, and freedom, forgive yourself and you may need to ask others for forgiveness, then move on. We all have needed to ask for forgiveness and had to forgive ourselves at some point, so you are not alone.

As you slowly heal, your inner light will begin to shine. Only positive results come from your inner light shining brightly. You were meant to shine! If you are struggling to feel great about yourself because of some mistakes that you have made, remember that we all make mistakes. You may be thinking right now that you will never forgive yourself for the terrible mistakes you made. This type of thinking will create self-hatred and put you in an emotional prison. The only way to set yourself free is by using the forgiveness key. You have access to that key each and every second of your life through your thoughts. One of the major differences between you and people who are living an extraordinary life may simply be that you have not forgiven yourself for your mistakes.

After you take yourself out of the emotional prison, then your self-abuse will end. If you set yourself up for pain and drama, you will clearly see that you have not forgiven yourself. Begin today to be free. You can do this by having compassion, understanding, and love toward yourself. You are human. Humans will err. Tell yourself over and over that you forgive yourself for your past mistakes, until you achieve forgiveness. If you do not take yourself out of your own emotional prison, then you are cheating everyone around you. You will be blocking your inner light because of your self-hatred. How can you soar in life when you are carrying an anchor of self-hatred that is holding you back? Cut the rope to this anchor, ask for forgiveness, forgive yourself and move forward.

Your light is meant to shine, so that you can make a positive difference in a world that is in great need of your help. You will not be healed if you continue to consciously or subconsciously beat yourself up. Great healing comes when you take ownership of your mistakes. Great results happen when you take any ugliness that was done to you or that you have done to others and turn that into goodness. What a victory to take darkness and transform it into light!

A healed person is someone who can also forgive others for their mistakes. You, too, will need to forgive anyone who has harmed you. It may feel nearly impossible to get to that point. You may be thinking right now, "I will never forgive that jerk for what he did." You may even secretly want the person who has harmed you to suffer for hurting you; therefore, you are not willing to move forward. The truth is, forgiveness is for you. When you do this, you are not saying that what someone did was right. What you are saying is that you will no longer be impacted by what that person did.

> *"Those who cannot forgive others*
> *break the bridge over which*
> *they themselves must pass."*
> *— Confucius*

When you hold on to anger, hatred, and resentment, you are only hurting yourself. Move through these feelings, so that you can be free. It is important to keep in mind that sometimes the people who harm us may end up blessing us the most. This has certainly happened throughout my life! The same is true with difficult situations. We sometimes get the greatest rewards from the most difficult situations!

After I go through something difficult, I will take time to think about how I benefited from that experience, even if someone tried to harm me. I have always been able to find some good in every situation. The same is true with you. If you focus on some of the good that is coming out of your difficult situation, this will help. How often have you focused on the good that came out of your difficult experiences? You are not alone! Most people never give this a thought. There is great freedom in knowing that you are not suffering just for the sake of it, but through your suffering you are being given a gift. Sometimes the only way to receive some amazing gifts is by going through difficult times. You may not be ready at this point to focus on anything good about having gone through your trials and tribulations, but once you are ready, give this some thought. Ask yourself, "What good am I receiving from this difficulty that I am experiencing?" Even though I never met you, I already know that you have grown and become stronger as a result of the difficulties you have faced. These two qualities will certainly serve you well throughout your life. I also know that once you get through your healing, you will appreciate life more than ever!

Linda started seeing me for counseling because all forty-eight years of her life had been "wonderful!" Yes, wonderful! Shortly after her aging parents experienced health issues, Linda began to have panic attacks. She was terrified that she would not be able to cope if she had to face any great losses or difficulties. Unfortunately, she was right. She never acquired any major coping skills that one would gain from experiencing a severe crisis, trauma, or loss. She intuitively knew that her cozy life had kept her from being strong, courageous, and having the ability to know that she will get through whatever life brings her way.

Linda is not alone. There are plenty of people who missed out on some of the major blessings that adversity has to offer. I have a dear friend who also experiences much anxiety because she is scared that she will not be able to cope if something major happens to her. She is like Linda. Her whole life was easy and good. It may be incomprehensible that some people can move through life without going through an ounce of what you have been through. However, once you are fully healed you will have a treasure trove of tools for the rest of your life! People who have never been in the hole missed the opportunity to find this treasure. Strength, courage, determination, wisdom, and appreciation are some of the gifts that come from climbing out of the hole of darkness.

Kimberly's father was extremely abusive toward her throughout her childhood. She never thought that she would be able to forgive him for the abuse, but she did. Kimberly realized that she had two choices in life: to remain miserable as a result of her trauma, or to live a great life and pursue her heart's desire of helping people who were suffering. She decided to heal herself so that she could help others. Kimberly said that if she did not suffer so much, then she never would have chosen her profession. If you make the choice of turning your pain into goodness, the rewards will be beyond your dreams.

Holding on to anger and resentment toward others will only block you from being open to more joy in your life. As I worked on my own forgiveness toward myself and others, I was more open to connecting with people from all walks of life. When I was in India, I sat on a big rock, as I faced the Indian Ocean. A man walked toward me and we started conversing. My very enjoyable conversation with this gentleman lasted for two hours. He told me that he was unhappy with his life. I offered encouraging words and he thanked me with sincere appreciation for helping him. I cannot say how enriched my life has been by simply talking and connecting with people from all walks of life. I find that most people are not willing to connect with others because of their own inner blocks. Not being willing to forgive yourself and others will become a major block that will stop you from being fully open to life and to people.

"There are people looking for exactly what you have to offer, and you are being brought together on the checkerboard of life."
— *Louise L. Hay*

If you take the time to connect with the people who are on your path, you will see that each person has something to offer you and that you have something to offer them. When I worked as a mental health consultant for two preschools, I watched how the preschoolers connected with each other so beautifully. They did not judge their classmates. They just enjoyed their new friends. These wonderful little beings were not blocked in any way. They were not holding on to anger toward anyone. A healed person is not only able to forgive, but can connect with people from all walks of life.

We never know how we are going to impact someone by connecting with them. We also do not know how we will be impacted by that experience. My favorite movie is *It's a Wonderful Life*. When you become who you are meant to be, then you are left wondering how many people you have touched and positively influenced. There will even be people you have positively impacted whom you will never meet. When you are kind to others, people will in turn be kind to those with whom they come in contact. Your kindness therefore has a ripple effect. Wow! That is the power of your inner light. Keep in mind that your inner light cannot shine brightly if you are unable to forgive and love yourself.

Michele's eighteen-year-old son died in the World Trade Center on September 11. The pain that Michele endured from her loss was absolutely horrific. My heart ached for her in every session. Many times throughout our work together, I tried very hard to hold back my tears. I knew that I had to fully support Michele with her feelings without focusing the sessions on my sadness about her loss and everyone else's loss on that dark day. After I counseled Michele for over one year, she said to me "I forgive the terrorists for murdering my son. I am not doing this for them, but for me. This is what I need to do in order to move forward." If Michele can forgive terrorists for taking her son's life, then you certainly can forgive yourself and others for past mistakes.

What do you need to forgive yourself for? I need to forgive myself for:

1._____

2._____

3._____

Whom do you need to forgive? I need to forgive:

1._____

2._____

3._____

I am now willing to forgive myself and others because:

_____

_____

_____

I will know when I have fully forgiven myself and others when:

_____

_____

_____

If you are angry about the thought of forgiving someone, then you have more healing to do before you can move forward. Remember, forgiveness is a gift that we give ourselves. Remind yourself that forgiveness does not mean that what someone did was right. It means that you have picked yourself up from the rubble and now you are able to move forward, stronger than ever! When you forgive, you are moving toward self-love.

CHAPTER 5

Meditating Can Transform Your Life

Meditating can help you with your healing process. It will allow you to get rid of negative feelings, become centered, de-stress, and change your state of mind. It will also powerfully help you to get in touch with your inner voice. The guidance that you receive from your inner voice will be remarkable! Making this connection is one of the best things you can do for yourself! One of the most beneficial tools to my own healing process and peace has been meditating. There were times when I needed to meditate several times a day in order to experience peace. I did not judge myself for using this tool whenever I needed it, nor do you need to judge yourself. If meditating works for you, then do it as often as you like.

Here are some other benefits to meditating:
- Improves your general health.
- Provides your cells with more oxygen and nutrients as you focus on particular body parts.
- Improves your body luster.
- Improves ability to focus.
- Increases creativity.
- Improves concentration.
- Decreases respiratory rate.
- Increases blood flow.

- Lowers blood pressure.
- Helps to slow the aging process.
- Increases productivity.
- Slows your heart rate.
- Helps to create a deep level of relaxation.
- Help to reduce anxiety attacks since it reduces the levels of blood lactate.
- Decreases headaches and muscle tension.
- Enhances your immune system.
- Has the potential to reduce the activity of viruses and emotional distress.
- Increases serotonin production, so that your mood and behavior will be more positive. Low levels of serotonin can produce depression, headaches, insomnia, and obesity.
- Increases the activity of natural-killer cells, which destroy bacteria and cancer cells.
- Can increase your confidence and self-esteem.

Did I fail to mention how beneficial meditating is for your body, mind, and spirit? I think from this list you get the point that meditating is highly beneficial.

When I was a teenager, I thought that people who meditated were silly. I remember being in a car with my mother and my aunt in the early 1980s; we saw two people who were meditating in their car. As a teenager, I could not help but laugh. I thought that those people were crazy. Little did I know how incredibly powerful meditating would be for my own life.

It is easy to dismiss something without giving it a try. You may think that it is silly to meditate, as I once thought. The silly thing would be for you not to do it, since the benefits are so profound!

There is no right or wrong way to meditate. You can simply relax and quiet your mind. There are many different ways and styles of meditating. Here are some of the most common: focusing/visualization meditation, listening, static transcendence, and mobile transcendence. I prefer to meditate by connecting with the unlimited wisdom that is available to all of us when you quiet your mind and tap into your intuition and by doing visualization work. If you are interested in learning more about these meditations, or many others, there are a plethora of books that you can read. It is important to discover what works best for you!

The *focusing meditation* involves focusing on something intently as a way of staying in the present moment and silencing your internal dialogue. You can try this little experiment. Light a candle and stay focused on the flame. When your thoughts wander, go back to focusing on the flame. As you do this, you will be controlling your thoughts and quieting your mind. With the *visualization meditation*, you are training your mind to focus in a certain direction. This is a great way to de-stress in a very short period of time.

The *listening or watching meditation* is a traditional Zen sitting meditation. Here you are just observing your thoughts, without trying to control them. The importance of this meditation is to hear divine guidance. The more you practice this meditation, the easier it will be to receive guidance.

The goal of the *static transcendence meditation* is to remove your thoughts completely. Yogis are known to do this form of meditation. It can literally take twenty years to master removing your thoughts. The yogis will use a mantra when they are meditating, such as Om or Aum. *Mobile transcendence* involves having the ability to enter a transcendental state, removing all thoughts, whenever you want.

> *"Whatever forms of meditation you practice, the most important point is to apply mindfulness continuously, and make a sustained effort. It is unrealistic to expect results from meditation within a short period of time. What is required is continuous sustained effort."*
> — *Dalai Lama*

For the purpose of this book, we will focus on going within and receiving intuitive information and doing visualization work. When I need clarity about anything, I will quickly quiet my mind and ask my intuition to reveal the answers to my questions. If I am not ready for an answer, then I will not receive one, but that rarely happens. When you go within and ask a question, you will receive an answer.

Quieting your mind is a great way to focus on the listening aspect. If your mind is racing, it will be much more challenging to receive intuitive information. If you find that you simply cannot quiet your mind even for one minute, then it may be best for you to do some visualization work before you go fully within. Any of the visualization techniques offered within this chapter will do the trick.

Sometimes before I meditate, I will jokingly think to myself, "It is now time to medicate." For me, meditating is like taking medication. My mind and body feel more relaxed and calm shortly after I close my eyes. If I am having a bad day, all I have to do is meditate and my state of being will change and I will feel great again. I do not make any major decisions without listening to my intuition. Even though I listen to my inner voice throughout my day, quieting my mind allows me to completely focus on my own answers, without any distractions. Therefore, I get very clear guidance. You may be thinking that this is a waste of time. Taking great care of yourself, especially as you heal, is not a waste of time!

> *"Meditation is painful in the beginning*
> *but it bestows immortal Bliss*
> *and Supreme joy in the end."*
> — *Swami Sivananda*

A great majority of people struggle with quieting their minds. The important thing is to start off slowly. Practice quieting your mind for one minute; gradually increase to two minutes, and so on. The way to do this is to sit or lie in a quiet place and simply focus on your breathing. When a thought enters your mind, bring your attention back to your breathing.

Another way that you can quiet your mind is by focusing on white light. See white light shine brightly on the top of your head. When your mind thinks about all those things that you need to get done, bring your attention back to the white light. It may take much practice before you fully master quieting your mind. Once you master this, you will feel great peace and joy. Not only will your mind and spirit benefit from meditating, but your body will, too.

When you quiet your mind, you can remove your ego so that your intuition can clearly guide your every step. Meditating is a great way to temporarily remove yourself from your ego, so that you receive invaluable information. When we fully focus on being still within, we are not only temporarily removing our egos but removing ourselves from everything. Therefore, you are giving yourself a mini-vacation, which will help you feel better. I do not know about you, but after I return from a relaxing vacation, I feel charged and my spirit is fueled to powerfully move forward in life. You have the ability to give yourself as many small vacations as you need throughout your day, even if they last for ten minutes. When you need a break from your feelings, these ten minutes will feel heavenly!

Ocean Meditation

Try this quick meditation to see how your state of mind can change in less than ten minutes. *To begin, sit or lie in a comfortable, quiet place. Slowly take three deep breaths in through your nose and out through your mouth. Allow your body to become completely relaxed. Gently close your eyes. You are now walking on the beach toward a bonfire. The bonfire has the power to destroy all your feelings and situations that are blocking you from feeling good. All your feelings and situations are now tightly packed in various suitcases that are behind you. You are going to slowly put your feelings and situations from each suitcase, one by one, in the bonfire. Do not be frightened by how many suitcases you see. Perhaps you have ten, fifty, or a hundred suitcases. It does not matter how many you have. What matters is that you get rid of them.*

Before you throw each suitcase in the fire, recognize what you are getting rid of. Perhaps you are getting rid of stress. How about sadness or anger? Is there a situation that has been causing you discomfort that you are ready to release? Get rid of everything that has been blocking you from being in a perfect state of peace. When you are ready, take the first suitcase and throw it in the fire. Hear the fire roar as it destroys everything. Focus on how good it feels to completely destroy what has been holding you back. Take a deep breath in through your nose and slowly exhale through your mouth. Grab the second suitcase. Acknowledge what you are getting rid of, then throw the suitcase in the fire. Keep doing this with each suitcase until they are all gone. Take your time getting rid of everything. Continue to slowly breathe in through your nose and exhale through your mouth.

Now that the suitcases are permanently destroyed, walk toward the ocean. The ocean is calm and peaceful. You cannot help but feel great. Sit on the sand as you face the ocean and notice that white light is completely surrounding your body. Take in the warmth and peace that this light has to offer. Now take in the joy that is yours for immersing yourself in this light. Allow yourself to fully absorb this light in your entire being. Once you have fully taken in this light, you are going to slowly come back in the room. Feel your feet on the floor. Hear any noises that exist in and outside of the room. Before you open your eyes, see the white light shining brightly from where you are sitting or lying. When you are ready, gently open your eyes.

Take a minute to become aware of how this simple meditation changed your state and decreased your stress.

This meditation helped me to:

_____

_____

_____

_____

"Meditation is the comfort in Life."
— ***Sri Sri Ravi Shankar***

Once you get in the habit of doing some form of meditation regularly, this will help you to de-stress and invite much peace in your life. The inner peace and joy that you experience from doing this will be well worth your time. This is one of the best things that you can give your body, mind, and spirit.

If you experience any stress or upset, this quick meditation can also change your state in less than ten minutes. Many of my patients have tried this meditation and they love it! Some of my patients even do this meditation with their children. Terry's eight-year-old daughter will often ask her mother to do it with her. After Terry and Grace do the meditation, Grace will tell her mother that she feels "so much better." Give it a try!

Hot Air Balloon Meditation

Think about what is currently keeping you from being in a good state. Perhaps you are experiencing difficult feelings, or you are going through a very difficult time. You may be experiencing much stress. You have financial problems. Your boss is being hard on you. You have too many demands placed on you. Now that you have identified what is keeping you in a lower state, get fully relaxed. Sit or lie in a comfortable place. *Slowly take in three deep breaths through your nose and out through your mouth. Gently close your eyes and see a big hot air balloon in front of you. Examine what the balloon looks like.*

When you are ready, begin to put all your thoughts, feelings, and situations that have been keeping you in this lower state in the hot air balloon. Notice the color of your thoughts, feelings, and situations that are holding you back from being peaceful and not feeling good. Slowly pour each of these things in the balloon, one at a time. The balloon is gradually becoming full. Keep releasing everything until the balloon is completely full.

Once the basket is full, pick up that remote control that is near your feet and hit the green button. The balloon is ascending toward the sky.

As soon as the hot air balloon is high in the sky, hit the red button. The hot air balloon is now exploding and everything you put in the balloon is being completely destroyed. It feels so good to get rid of the feelings and situations that were keeping you stuck in a lower state. See yourself running with great joy and happiness now that you are free. You are free from all those feelings and situations that were negatively impacting you. You are free from everything! Take in the joy even more from being totally free. When you are ready, begin to come back in the room. Feel your feet on the floor. Become aware of any noises that are in the room and gently open your eyes. Notice how quickly your state has changed by doing this simple technique.

This meditation helped me to:

_____

_____

_____

Another meditation that I often use with my patients in order to help them to quickly change their state is what I call the White Light technique. *After Ron's twenty-four-year-old daughter, Paris, passed away from an automobile accident, he didn't think he would ever feel peaceful or happy again. He was desperate to heal and sought my help. For many sessions in our work together, he just mourned and grieved his lost daughter, but slowly he began to see glimmers of how his life might go on from here.*

The White Light Meditation was a particularly powerful tool for Ron. In this exercise you visualize what's stopping you from being at peace and then picture yourself releasing it, maybe through a hot air balloon or down through your feet. Once you detach yourself from what is upsetting, your body feels the impact. Then you visualize a heavenly white light and experience a state of deep peace.

Many times throughout our work together, Ron would sob, then manage to catch his breath and quietly ask, "Do you mind if we do the white light thing?" This simple meditative practice proved to be a major factor in moving him toward peace and healing. "Even though I still feel sad at times," he told me in our last session, "I am fine with those moments of sadness."

White Light Meditation

To begin, slowly take three deep breaths in through your nose and out through your mouth. With each breath that you take in, you are going to become more relaxed. See a hose going through your feet down to the middle of the earth that is on fire. Become aware of what is keeping you from being in a good state in the form of a color. Let this color move through your body and into the hose. The fire is going to completely destroy whatever has been keeping you stuck in a lower state. You are now getting rid of any feelings, situations, or stress that have been blocking you from feeling good.

See these things leave your body as they are being fully destroyed by the fire. After you release everything that has been keeping you in a lower state, release the hose and see a white light come down from the sky and completely surround your body. This light is replacing what you just got rid of with love, peace, and joy. Absorb as much of this as you need. The light is becoming brighter as it touches every fiber of your being. The light is filling your heart with even more peace and comfort. Keep taking in the healing power that this light has to offer. It feels so good to immerse yourself in this light. You are going to slowly take a deep breath in through your nose and exhale through your mouth. As you take in a deep breath, you are going to breathe in the light and exhale the light through your body. The light is now even brighter. See beautiful rays of light come down from the sky and completely surround your entire being. The light just got brighter. Allow your body to take in the light even more. Each cell of your body is absorbing this light. Your whole body is completely relaxed and at peace. Take in as much of this light for as long as you can.

When you are ready, you are going to slowly come back in the room. See the white light surround your body where you are sitting. Become aware of any noises that are in the room. Slowly move your fingers and toes. When you are ready, gently open your eyes.

This meditation helped me to:

_____

_____

_____

Many of my patients have told me that they felt really peaceful and good after doing this meditation. As you move through your healing process, you may benefit from doing this exercise every day. In fact, you may want to do it several times a day if you are experiencing a severe crisis, trauma, or loss. If Ron was able to experience moments of peace from doing the white light meditation, then so can you. Be kind to yourself and meditate as often as you can. There truly is no excuse for not having the time to meditate when it only takes ten minutes to do any one of these three techniques.

Tapping in to Your Intuition

Once you have mastered these techniques, you may want to try to get answers directly from your intuition. You will need to quiet your mind for as long as you can. Make sure that you are fully relaxed.

Slowly take three deep breaths in through your nose and out through your mouth. Surround yourself with white light. Stay completely focused on seeing this light. Once you are able to quiet your mind and completely focus on the white light, begin to ask your intuition a question. Patiently wait for an answer. The answer will appear in your own mind through your thoughts.

Take in another deep breath through your nose and exhale through your mouth. Keep focusing on the light and silence your mind as much as you can, then ask your next question. Take your time to listen to your inner voice. Take another deep breath in through your nose and slowly exhale through your mouth. See the white light get even brighter, and ask your final question. After you receive your answer, you are going to take one more deep breath in through the nose and exhale through the mouth. You are now going to slowly come back in the room. Feel your feet on the floor and open your eyes.

This meditation helped me:

_____

_____

_____

The information that I received from this meditation was:

_____

_____

_____

I have been consistently meditating for the past fourteen years. The benefits that I have received from meditating have been remarkable. Whenever I want to quickly change my state, all I have to do is meditate. The more I meditate, the more beneficial this is to me. The guidance that I receive from meditating is priceless. If someone told me twenty years ago how much meditating could positively impact my life, I NEVER would have believed them. From counseling hundreds of patients over the years and getting so much positive feedback, I can tell you that you will be glad to make meditating a part of your life.

Do not get discouraged if you have trouble visualizing or getting intuitive information. I had trouble getting intuitive information for many years. I just kept practicing. Now, I can get information unbelievably quickly and easily. Some of my patients had trouble visualizing anything; but the more they practiced, the more they were able to do so. Several of my patients mentioned that they were worried they were not doing the meditations right. Do not worry about whether you are doing them right. The more you practice, the better you will be at it. Stop judging yourself as you meditate. Just allow your experience to happen.

> ***"The affairs of the world will go on forever.***
> ***Do not delay the practice of meditation."***
> *— Milarepa*

Now that I have discovered that meditating is beneficial, I am going to make a commitment to:

_____

_____

Meditating is a skill. Like any skill, the more you do it, the better you will be at it. Keep practicing until this becomes a natural part of your life. Meditation is one of the most beneficial skills that you can possibly develop. The wonderful thing about meditating is that you can do it at any time! This amazing skill is going to change your life forever once you master it! Meditating is one of the very few things that you can do in less than ten minutes to de-stress, change your state, and feel peaceful.

PART III

Claiming Your Happiness

CHAPTER 6

How to Be Happy

"Happiness is a habit—cultivate it."
— *Elbert Hubbard*

No matter where you are in life, being happy takes work. What has been hindering your happiness over the past couple of years? Do you emotionally beat yourself up? You cannot abuse yourself and be happy at the same time. You may not even be aware of how much you beat yourself up. Over the next few days, become aware of what you think and say to yourself. You may notice that you can be emotionally abusive toward yourself by your thoughts and words. This ugly habit can be changed by getting in the good habit of speaking kindly to yourself.

Not only do your positive thoughts and words need to support your happiness, but your behavior needs to support your happiness as well. If you are doing things that make you feel terrible, then you are sabotaging your happiness. The more you make decisions that feel right to you and you know are right, the happier you will become. It is your responsibility to make good decisions that add to your life, not make you feel lousy about yourself.

I have worked with many people who had happiness at their fingertips; however, they kept abusing themselves through their thoughts, words, and actions. Beating the happiness out of you is useless. Throw away the bat at this moment. See the emotional bat fly out the nearest window. Stop holding yourself hostage by treating yourself so poorly!

Anita is a successful doctor. She is talented, smart, and people genuinely like her. Whenever Anita is ready to experience a whole new level of happiness, she will do everything to sabotage her happiness. Anita had been dating Mike for two years and she was ready to get married. She desperately wanted to start a family since she was almost thirty-eight. When Mike was ready to propose to her, she started finding fault with everything he did. She even decided not to go away with him because she was too angry that he had not proposed to her on Valentine's Day.

Mike told Anita a couple of weeks later that he had planned on proposing to her on their vacation. He was crushed that she ruined something he had been dreaming of for the past two years. Anita continued this negative pattern of sabotaging her happiness until I helped her to clearly see her behavior. She then began to understand why she sabotages other great things in her life as well. Her guilt over having made some poor choices in the past was at the root of her destructive behavior. Are you like Anita? Do you sabotage your happiness?

> **"Expect the best; convert problems into opportunities;**
> **be dissatisfied with the status quo; focus on where you want**
> **to go, instead of where you're coming from; and most importantly,**
> **decide to be happy, knowing it's an attitude, a habit gained from daily**
> **practice, and not a result or payoff."**
> **— Denis Waitley**

Perhaps you are abusing yourself because someone else abused you in the past. You may have unconsciously continued this pattern since it is familiar to you. It is sad that you were emotionally beat up. However, you need to realize that the past is over. Today, you have the power to destroy your bat! Keep supporting yourself with being loving and kind to yourself until this becomes familiar. People often attract others who treat them the way they were treated in the past or the way they are currently treating themselves. This will continue until you change your pattern. If you are loving and kind to yourself, you certainly would not tolerate someone mistreating you. If you abuse yourself, then you are likely to accept someone else's abuse.

Your journey toward becoming healed is going to be more enjoyable if you make a commitment to be kind to yourself from today forward. You have the power to change your thoughts, actions, and behaviors toward yourself at this very moment. You need to start seeing the good that lies within. You are just as valuable as anyone on earth! You have a purpose in life that only you can fulfill. It is important to like and love yourself so that you can fulfill your purpose. The more you like yourself, the easier it will be to like others. Have you ever noticed that some people are negative and critical about everyone they meet? This is a result of not liking who they are. They are stuck with focusing on the things they do not like about themselves; therefore, they zoom in on anything they do not like about others.

Some of the most loving people on earth have the ability to see their own inner beauty; therefore, they automatically see the beauty in everyone they meet. How about you? Do you judge and criticize others in your mind, or do you focus on what you like about them? Do you realize that people will not feel good being around you if you are criticizing them, even in your own mind? The converse is also true. If you have positive thoughts about others, this positive energy will make people want to be around you.

One mistake I have made throughout my life is that I allowed others to take away from my happiness. I am genuinely happy for people when they are happy, so I thought that everyone would support me in my happiness. Before I learned that there would be people who could not support my happiness, I shared my happiness with everyone I knew. This was a big mistake I kept making over and over! As a result of continuing to make that mistake, I felt drained by people who were unable to support my happiness. It was disappointing to discover that not everyone was able to support me the way that I was able to support them. There is some truth to the saying that "Misery loves company."

It is important to know who will be able to support you and who cannot. Do not allow anyone to take away from you in any way. Some people may not even be aware of their subconscious desire to dismantle your happiness. If you do not have people in your life who can support your happiness, then it is time to make new friends. There are plenty of wonderful people in this world who will gladly celebrate your happiness with you. In order for this to happen, you need to make room for this support.

"A true friend knows your weaknesses but shows you your strengths; feels your fears but fortifies your faith; sees your anxieties but frees your spirit; recognizes your disabilities but emphasizes your possibilities."
— *William Arthur Ward*

Years ago when I was doing an internship, I heard two women gossip about the director, myself, and everyone they could possibly gossip about. At that time, I truly could not understand how someone could be somewhat pleasant when they spoke to you and so hurtful when they thought you were not listening. Now, I see that experience differently. Some people who are hurting on the inside may feel a need to gossip and be hurtful. Other people's happiness stirs up their internal mess that they live with daily. Even though it is sad to know that people are hurting, I stay away from negativity as much as possible. When you do not accept people's negativity, you are no longer contributing to their unhealthiness.

"Good character is a prerequisite to happiness.
It entails empathy, courage, generosity,
work, honesty, discipline, and balance.
It is not easily achieved.
It is not a lesson which can be learned from books.
It requires practice."
— *Jeane J. Kirkpatrick*

If you have been the one who has been gossiping, then forgive yourself and work on doing some internal healing, so that you no longer continue this ugly way of being. If someone is gossiping daily, then this is a clear sign that they are not able to support your happiness. You will find that healthy people can easily celebrate all your successes and happiness with you. This will give them great pleasure. There will be people in your life who may never choose to heal, yet they will also be able to support your happiness. Take a few minutes to become fully aware of which people will support you.

The people currently in my life who will fully support my happiness are:

1. _____
2. _____
3. _____
4. _____
5. _____

How are you going to fully support yourself? I am going to support my happiness by:

_____
_____
_____
_____

One of the biggest responsibilities that we have in life is to make ourselves happy. People often fail to realize that it is not anyone's job to make you happy. This is fully your job. Most people like to blame others for their unhappiness. "I cannot believe that my life turned out this way because of you. If my parents had only pushed me more, then my life would have been good." Blaming someone for your unhappiness will get you nowhere. If you continue to blame others, then you will be stuck in misery.

People can certainly add to your life, but they cannot make you happy. Happiness comes from within. When you are in the tunnel, your focus needs to be on taking one step at a time to get through this difficult time in your life. If you do experience glimpses of happiness as you heal, savor them and make them last as long as you can. If your happiness lasts for five minutes, discover how you can make it last for ten minutes.

Even though true happiness comes from within, there are things you can do to create more of it for yourself. Discover various ways that you can do this, and then take action. If you do not know what makes you happy, then remove this block by making a list of everything new that you would like to try. Make it a point to do all the things on your list. Become aware of how great you feel by adding more good to your life. Think about some things from your childhood that made you happy. There is nothing wrong with incorporating things from childhood back in your life as an adult. You are the only one who will be able to give yourself what you once loved.

Throughout my life, my heart would jump for joy whenever I heard piano music. Instead of cheating myself out of my childhood passion, I signed up for piano lessons. I now have been taking lessons for a couple of years. I enjoy playing my piano. I could have easily talked myself out of creating more happiness for myself by thinking, "My life is so busy, I do not have time to learn how to play the piano. It is too late for me to take lessons. I am too old." I was not willing to continue to make excuses. Life is too short not to be fully happy!

How can you add happiness in your life? I can add happiness in my life by:

_____

_____

_____

_____

_____

Now take a few minutes to see yourself doing the things you listed. How does it feel to incorporate them into your life? Hold on to those feelings for a few minutes. Experiencing greater happiness is not only going to benefit you; it will also impact other people's lives as well. The happier you are, the more your inner light will shine and positively impact everyone around you. What excuses are you going to make for not adding happiness in your life? When are you going to move beyond your excuses?

Once you are healed and happy, you will have a powerful impact on people, without even trying. The same is true with very negative people. They can have a powerful negative impact on people, without trying to.

Have you ever noticed how uncomfortable it is to be around someone who is very negative and settled in living a life of misery? Yes, it is very uncomfortable. Even little children become uncomfortable being around someone who has chosen misery. We can choose happiness or choose misery by staying stuck in life. You would not be reading this book if you did not already make the choice to live a life of victory! The happier you are the more you will have to give to others; therefore, everyone benefits. Your happiness awaits you—claim it!

You may be thinking that you will never be happy again because of what you are going through. Not true! There have been many people on this earth who have experienced exactly what you are currently experiencing, and they are happy today. Why not do a little research and see if you can talk to some of these people? This may help you to see that the sun can be shining in your life again soon!

CHAPTER 7

Develop a Great Attitude

"A happy person is not a person in a certain set of circumstances, but rather a person with a certain set of attitudes."
— *Hugh Downs*

Now that you have made a commitment to be happy, it is important to develop a great attitude! This is another key requirement to being happy and it certainly will make the journey toward becoming healed much brighter. When you are experiencing deep emotions, it will be challenging to have a good attitude. However, when you take those lemons that life throws at you and make lemonade, your great attitude will surely make your healing process and any situation better.

Do you know that you can actually experience inner joy in the middle of some difficult situation? The amount of joy that you experience in any given situation is directly related to your attitude. Several years ago after my hot water heater broke and water flowed through my kitchen and living room, I remained joyful and happy on the inside. Instead of focusing on everything that was going wrong, I focused on how blessed I was to have an old friend who came to help me at 2:00 in the morning.

My friend and I laughed after every phone call I made to various plumbers who guaranteed that they would be at your house in thirty minutes if your hot water heater burst. All seven plumbers told me that they would not be at my house until the morning. So much for their guarantee! I did not need their help in the morning; I needed their help as water continued to gush out of my hot water heater. The fact that people advertised in the phone book that they would be there within thirty minutes and were not true to their word was so absurd that my friend and I found it hilarious. By the seventh and last phone call, we were practically falling on the floor with laughter. I could have easily had a negative attitude, especially since I had had many other things go wrong with my house that year, but I refused to do that. The most important end result from that experience was that my friend and I were able to bond more than we had that whole year.

Instead of being negative when something goes wrong, I ask myself, "How can I make lemonade out of this situation?" When was the last time you asked yourself this question? Whenever I have to wait for an appointment that I normally would not have to wait for, I will make lemonade: I will use that time wisely, rather than be annoyed about having to wait. The rewards that come from having a good attitude are amazing. Not only will you feel good, but your results will be positive.

When Sarah felt she was in the tunnel, a branch fell on the roof of her car during a bad storm. Sarah was too overwhelmed to immediately fix her car, even though her insurance company gave her $2,000 for the damages. Sarah knew that she would get her car fixed as soon as she was no longer overwhelmed by life. What she did not know at that time was that it actually would cost her over $3,600 to repair her roof. A few months after the branch damaged her car, someone accidentally hit the rear door of her car while it was parked at a train station. Unfortunately, she never discovered who hit her parked car; therefore, she was left with having to pay another $500 toward her collision deductible for the new damage.

Sarah is known for having a great attitude, even while experiencing much inner turmoil. It is very easy for her to make lemonade out of any situation. Sarah told herself that something good was going to happen as a result of her good attitude. Sure enough, something good did happen. Sarah mentioned to a local mechanic what had happened to her car. The mechanic told her to go to a local auto body shop and tell them that Henry sent her. She immediately went to the auto body shop and explained her situation. She was then told that they would repair ALL the damage on her car for a little more than what her insurance company gave her and that she would not have to pay anything for the new damage! Sarah knew that she was being rewarded for her good attitude! When you have a good attitude, people will go out of their way to help you!

What we tell ourselves about a situation will determine how we feel. If you remain positive and know that something great will come out of your situation, then it will. If you are angry and negative about being handed lemons, then you cannot make lemonade. You will feel down and discouraged. A positive attitude will help you to make great choices that will lead to positive results. A negative attitude will block you from seeing all your options in any given situation.

By developing a positive attitude, you may suddenly discover that it is easy to make new friends. People enjoy being around someone with a good attitude. Take a few minutes to think about someone you know who has a positive attitude. How do you feel when you are around that person? Of course you feel good and energized just by being in that person's presence. That is how people will feel when they are around you once your attitude is positive.

> *"The greatest discovery of my generation is that man can alter his life simply by altering his attitude of mind."*
> — *James Truslow Adams*

When you feel great about yourself and have a good attitude, you will automatically be in a good state. Therefore, you cannot help but feel great. When your state is not good, as a result of a poor attitude, stress, and minor annoyances, you will feel lousy. As you heal, your state will fluctuate. Do not expect yourself to be in a constant good state. This is not realistic when you have overwhelming emotions that need to be felt. You can fully focus on being in a good state when you are no longer overwhelmed by your feelings and your situation.

There are many things that you can do to quickly change your state. Moving your body is a great way to accomplish this. How do you like to move your body? Do you enjoy dancing to music? After you do this for only fifteen minutes, you will feel great. Nature is another fast way to help you feel refreshed and good. Listening to something inspirational will do the same. Thinking positively and believing what you are saying can quickly help you. Keeping yourself in a good state is a must in order for your attitude to remain positive. Do your best to do things that help you feel good as often as possible throughout each day. This will greatly help you as you heal. As with anything, keep working at this until you master being in a good state, so that you can have a great attitude every day.

Take a few minutes to think about some possible ways that you can put yourself in a good state. The three ways that I can put myself in a good state are by:

1._____
2._____
3._____

Most people's states will quickly change after exercising. Is that on your list? If not, add that to your list. Eating well will also help you to be in a good state. If you currently do not eat well, you have another thing to add to your list. Give yourself the gift of letting go of whatever is keeping you from being in a good state. Remember, even as you heal, you can temporarily give yourself moments of peace. When you are in a good state, your mind will be clearer and it will be easier to listen to your intuition.

It is often wise to put yourself in a good state before you make any major decisions. You will then be able to clearly recognize what you want and what is best for you. If you make a decision when you are in a bad state, you may end up regretting it. If you are not ready to decide something, buy yourself some time by saying, "I need to think about that, but I will get back to you soon."

Keep working at this on a regular basis. Experiment and discover how you can quickly change your state and keep yourself in that good place. Keep in mind that what helps others to remain in a good state may not necessarily work for you. Discover what works best for you!

People often underestimate how important it is to think positively. This is one of the key requirements to having a good attitude and to being peaceful, happy, and living an extraordinary life. When your thoughts are positive, your feelings and actions will be as well. Negative thinking only creates stress and turmoil. It also produces negative feelings, actions, and outcomes. This is certainly not what you want. You cannot be at your best if your thoughts are negative. You can have a fantastic life and be miserable due to your thoughts. The reverse is also true; you may have a very difficult life and be happy due to your positive thinking.

> *"Most of us are about as happy*
> *as we make our minds up to be."*
> *— Abraham Lincoln*

When you are going through any type of trial or tribulation, it will be very challenging to keep your thoughts positive. I sometimes find myself struggling with this after I encounter a stressful situation. However, I push myself to think positively even though it takes some effort at that point. Once I quickly get back on track, I feel good and I am able to let go of the emotional attachment to the situation. Therefore, I am able to free myself from unpleasant feelings.

For some, thinking negatively is so automatic that they do not even realize that their thoughts and words are hurting them. They are so used to thinking this way that it may seem nearly impossible to reprogram their mind. Is this an ugly habit of yours as well? Perhaps you have been doing this for many years. The good news is that you can break this habit once and for all. I know that it will take some effort on your part to reprogram your thinking, but your effort will pay off!

Some of my patients tell me quite frequently what a challenge it is for them to do this. Okay, but keep at it anyway until it becomes automatic. You will struggle with this at first, but over time it will get easier. Before you know it, most of your thoughts will be positive. When your thoughts add to your life, this is another way that you can be loving and kind to yourself. If you are struggling to keep your thoughts positive, then give yourself ten minutes a day to have all those nasty negative thoughts. After the ten minutes are up, you will need to shift your focus toward thinking positively.

> *"We are what we think. All that we are arises*
> *With our thoughts. With our thoughts,*
> *We make our world."*
>
> — ***The Buddha***

Last year, Anne was in the tunnel after her marriage of twenty-one years ended. Her husband's infidelity made her feel that she was worthless and not good enough. Anne thought that she was never going to feel good again as a result of her suffering. Throughout her healing, she fully felt her feelings, kept her thoughts positive, and took positive action to do things she loves. In less than two years, Anne went from total despair to feeling great about herself and her life. Her eyes are now glowing! She is no longer the same woman she was when I first met her. Anne makes choices that fully add to her life. It would have been easy for her to stay stuck in misery if she were not willing to heal, grow, and completely change her thinking. However, she made the conscious choice of wanting to be happy and healed. All of Anne's healing paid off because she is now happier than ever!

When was the last time you dwelled on the positive things in your life? Has this idea ever occurred to you? Probably not! A great majority of people dwell on the negative. When was the last time you thought about a compliment that someone gave you that made you feel good? Did you think about that for a few seconds and quickly let it go? Of course you did! What about the negative comments or remarks that you heard, did you hold on to them? Of course you did! You ruminated on them over and over in your mind. You are not alone. Do you remember all the compliments you received over the past couple of years? Probably not! You were not conditioned to hold on to the good. Instead, you hold on to the negative and feel lousy.

How would your life be different if you dwelled on the positives? You guessed it; your life would be more peaceful and happy. What we focus on in life is what we will have more of. If you focus on the negative, then you will experience more of this. Not only will what we focus on expand, but we will be giving what we focus on POWER. If you simply focus on one thing in your life that is not right, you are giving this negative power. Therefore, you will have more unwanted outcomes. Why not stay focused on positive things in your life, so that you can create more of what you want?

> *"May you live all the days of your life."*
> *— Jonathan Swift*

Compliment Journal

One way to dwell on the positives is by fully focusing on them. How about focusing on all the compliments you receive over the next month? You probably receive more compliments than you realize. Why not treat yourself to a compliment journal? At the end of this book, I have provided a way for you to keep track of the compliments that you receive over the next 30 days. Every time you receive a compliment, write exactly what was said to you. This can be a lot of fun. On the days when you do not receive a compliment, give one to yourself. Review your journal often. By keeping a compliment journal, you will be holding on to the good and creating fantastic feelings about yourself in the process. This will help to reinforce that you are worthy and valuable. When you see this truth within yourself, you will be more open to unlimited possibilities.

There is great power in positive thinking and in dwelling on the positives. Not only will you feel better, but your outcomes will add to your life! If you want to see how powerful your thoughts truly are, talk to a few people who have accomplished something fantastic. They will tell you that the number one key ingredient to their success had to do with their positive thinking. Your positive thinking and your good state of mind will continue to support your great attitude and send you on your way toward happiness unlike ever before!

CHAPTER 8

How to Develop Your Intuition

"Intuition is a spiritual faculty and does not explain, but simply points the way."
— *Florence Scovel Shinn*

Our intuition speaks to us all the time, but we sometimes fail to listen. The more you listen to your intuition, the more you will be guided toward living a life filled with great joy and peace. The fact that you are reading this right now shows that you are ready to develop your intuition. Good for you! This is one of the greatest gifts you can have.

How many people really listen to their inner voice? When you were a small child, your inner voice was loud and clear. While you were growing up, you may have been told, "No, that is not right; do not do that. What were you thinking? You should not feel that way." After you get told enough times that what you were thinking and feeling is wrong, you learn not to trust your inner voice; therefore it gets buried. As the years go by, you lose touch with your intuition even more.

This is exactly what happened to me during my childhood. I was constantly told I was wrong whenever I shared an intuitive thought, or any thought. I can still hear my father telling me to go out and play, rather than talk to me. By the age of five, I learned to bury my inner voice as much as possible. One year after my father passed away, when I was fifteen, my intuition automatically resurfaced. Perhaps it came to life since my father was no longer making me feel wrong for having an inner voice. At that time, I was clueless as to why I knew things but could not explain how I knew them. It was not until my early twenties that I learned that my intuition was speaking to me and guiding me.

People often ignore their intuition because following it might mean having to change some aspect of their life that is not working. Change is scary for most people. Being happy in the end will be worth any changes you need to make. Trust your intuition and get ready to embrace peace and happiness unlike anything you have ever experienced in your life! The more you listen to your intuition, the louder it will become. The louder it becomes, the easier it will be to move through life with greater confidence. You cannot help but be confident when you know and trust that you are being perfectly guided on your journey.

How many times have you gotten yourself in a difficult situation because you did not listen to your inner voice? The consequences from not listening can have a negative impact on your life. Some of my patients have said, "I wish that I would have listened to my intuition. If I did, then I would never have gotten into this mess." It is easy to rationalize your inner voice, so that you can get what you want, rather than what is truly good for you. That mistake can be costly.

Mary was attracted to Fred, a charming younger man, but after only a month of dating he became verbally abusive. He wanted to control every move she made and was jealous of any male friends. Her instincts told her that Fred was not good for her, yet she married him nonetheless, swept up in something that seemed more powerful than her inner voice. Marriage did nothing to quell Fred's abusive behavior. She found the strength to leave him after six months, by which time she was pregnant. Her son is a great blessing, but he keeps Mary tied in a tumultuous relationship to her ex-husband. They are constantly arguing, yelling, and hanging up on each other, leaving Mary feeling "sick and miserable." They can't seem to agree on even the smallest details of Benjamin's schedule, and more than once they have battled it out in court. Mary vows she will "never, ever" ignore her inner voice again.

> *"Trust your hunches. They're usually based on facts filed away just below the conscious level."*
> *— Joyce Brothers*

Your intuition can literally save your life. Patty almost died a couple of years ago when her sodium levels fell drastically. Patty is health-conscious. She makes sure that she drinks plenty of water, eats well, and exercises regularly. She decided to change her diet to include foods very low in sodium. One month later, she was rushed to the hospital. She felt as though her body were going through some form of electric shock. She also experienced a panic attack for the first time in her life, which was the result of her extremely low sodium levels. She knew that something was terribly wrong and that she was either going to have a seizure or die if she did not get to a hospital. That was her intuition speaking to her loud and clear.

On that day, she happened to be spending time with a new friend who was a nurse at a local hospital. At first, Patty thought that her friend knew better than she did about whether she should go to the hospital. As Jan witnessed Patty hyperventilate, shake, vomit, and experience terrible pain, she thought that Patty was having a severe panic attack that would pass. Patty decided to listen to her inner voice and go to the hospital. The doctors told her that she could have died from her extremely low level of sodium. One doctor was surprised that she hadn't had a seizure. Even though Patty doubted her inner voice at first, the doctors confirmed that her intuition was right. Patty was very blessed by listening to her inner voice. If she did not take action, she could have died. If Patty could listen to her intuition when she was near death, there is no excuse for you not to listen to yours!

You may be out of practice with listening to your intuition, but YOU ARE INTUITIVE! If you are not in the habit of listening, then this will take some effort on your part. Practice until you can do this easily. All your efforts will be worth experiencing the good that comes from having your inner voice guide you each day. Listening to, trusting, and believing your intuition are three of the most powerful tools you will ever have in life.

"Follow your instincts.
That's where true
wisdom manifests itself."
— Oprah Winfrey

Your intuition will guide you toward doing what is best for you at any given moment. How would your life be different if you always listened to your intuition?

If I always listened to my intuition, then:

_____

_____

Your life would certainly be filled with more inner peace and happiness. You would no longer doubt what you think is best for you. Only *you* know what is best for you! The only time that this may not be true is if you are emotionally unstable. If that is the case, reach out to professionals and loved ones for a temporary guiding hand.

What is stopping you from fully listening to your intuition?

_____

_____

_____

_____

Eleanor is a forty-six-year-old woman who was offered an administrative job that she intuitively knew was not right for her. She dismissed her intuition and accepted the position that everyone told her she "should" take. Eleanor woke up every morning feeling sick to her stomach because she dreaded going to work. For nine months, she desperately wanted to quit, but did not want to "let anyone down." Eleanor knew that she was paying a high price for not following her intuition. She told me that she wished she could just honor her inner voice, without feeling as though she had to please everyone.

Does this sound familiar? Do you let people tell you what is right for you, even when your gut is screaming, "No, this is not right for me"? I was guilty of letting significant people in my life persuade me in the wrong direction for many years. I now listen to and follow my intuition almost all the time.

If I had not listened to my intuition when I was twenty, my whole life would be completely different at this moment. My friend at that time, Lisa, advised me not to take out student loans because I would be in debt for the rest of my life. The scholarship that I received at that time was certainly not enough to cover my tuition, so I knew that the only way for me to accomplish my goal of earning a Bachelor's degree was to take out loans. Even though I was heavily influenced by Lisa's opinion, my intuition clearly let me know that I did need to take out loans and trust that I would be able to pay them off someday.

My intuition was right. A few years after I earned my degree, I was able to fully pay off all my student loans. If I had taken my friend's advice and failed to listen to my intuition, then I would still be working at a job that paid very little and made me miserable. Thank goodness for my intuition! My education has allowed me to make a good living and do what I love!

I have to admit that once or twice a year I will ignore my inner voice when it comes to small things. After I dishonor myself by not listening, I am immediately reminded that I need to listen to my intuition in even the smallest circumstances.

A few years ago, I visited my dear friend, Mogan, who lives in Texas. After my visit with her and her family, her husband dropped me off at the airport. He firmly said to me, "Bring your luggage on the plane; it will be much easier than checking it." My intuition for some reason was telling me that that was not right for me, but I did not know why. I told him, "No, I think I will check my luggage." He adamantly said one more time, "Just take it on board. It will be easier that way." I knew that Joe had good intentions, so I temporarily put myself in the people-pleasing mode, which is something I rarely do anymore, and agreed.

As I was going through security with my one piece of luggage and my carry-on, a tall, scruffy-looking guy harshly asked, "Whose bag is this?" I knew that I had done nothing wrong, so I confidently said, "It is mine." I was immediately told that I needed to put my luggage back on the belt and that it needed to go through the scanner one more time. The security officer said that I had to go to the end of the line again. After I waited on the long line, I put my luggage on the belt one more time. Once again, I was harshly asked, "Whose luggage is this?" After I said that the luggage was mine, I was asked if it was okay if they searched the contents. I said, "Sure." Once the man realized that I was completely comfortable with him examining my luggage, he calmed down and apologized to me for having to do so.

While he was rummaging through my luggage, he pulled out one of my favorite hair products. I was then instructed to either check my luggage or throw out all my liquids. I certainly did not want to discard my favorite hair products and perfume, so I had to check the luggage after all after which I had to go on the long line and start the whole security process for the THIRD time! The extra amount of time that it took me to go through this process almost caused me to miss my flight.

If I had honored my intuition, I would have saved myself much stress and a wait on three long lines! This small experience reminded me that even though most people have good intentions, there is no way for them to know what is best for me. The same is true for you. People may have good intentions, but there is no way for them to know what is best for you. Your intuition will clearly tell you what is best for you at all times.

How have you been impacted by not following your intuition? How do you get in touch with your intuition? The most powerful way for me to get in touch with my intuition is through meditating. I get very valuable intuitive information throughout my day; however, when I am quiet and completely relaxed, it is easier for me to listen to my inner voice. Once you fully develop your intuition, you will be more confident not only in yourself, but also in your decisions.

For years, I prayed that I would be very intuitive. This was something that I craved. The way I developed my intuition was by testing the information I received. I would go into a meditation and ask many questions, such as, "What do I need to know? What do I need to focus on today?" The answers I receive are always valuable. Again, it did take me quite awhile to develop my intuition, so be patient with yourself. As with any skill, the more you practice, the more you are going to get results.

Have you ever gotten lost while you were driving? This can be stressful and aggravating. When you have a navigator, you are easily guided to where you want to go. Your intuition is your navigator. It will guide you perfectly. Your intuition will not fail you. It cannot possibly fail you. Your job is to listen and follow through with the guidance you receive.

Another great way to begin to slowly tap into your intuition is by paying close attention to your inner world. Most people are so focused on what is occurring in their outer world that they fail to listen within. Take a few minutes each day to check in with yourself. See how you feel about the small things in life. When you get a small gut reaction, know that this is your intuition speaking to you. It is important to pay close attention to those reactions. Once I help my patients to listen to their inner voice, they very often tell me that they think their intuition is one of the greatest tools they have in life. My sentiments exactly!

When was the last time you got in touch with that special place within yourself that has all your answers? Perhaps this is new for you. Over the next week, why not try this exercise to help you to get in touch with that special place within? You can begin this process by paying close attention to how you feel in each interaction. Your intuition will speak to you through your feelings. Notice what feels right and does not feel right to you. When someone asks you to do something, become aware of how you feel. If something is not right for you, honor yourself by saying no. Your intuition is there to serve you. The only way you can fully let it serve you is by honoring what you know is right for you. As you pay close attention to your intuition over the next week, take some time to write about your experience. This will help to turn up the volume of your inner voice even more.

Writing Exercise: Turning Up the Volume of Your Inner Voice

Day 1. Today, I focused on my intuition by:

_____

_____

Day 2. I focused on my intuition even more today when:

_____

_____

Day 3. I intuitively felt that:

_____

_____

Day 4. My intuition is now showing me that:

_____

_____

Day 5. Today my intuition helped me to:

_____

_____

Day 6. I checked in with my intuition today when:

_____

_____

Day 7. I intuitively felt that:

_____

_____

> *"The only real valuable thing is intuition."*
> *— Albert Einstein*

Allow your intuition to help you have clarity with things that create turmoil, confusion, or any negative feelings. Your intuition will shed light on these areas and help you. If you ignore your intuition, you are likely to stay stuck in negative situations and feelings. You and your intuition need to work together. Now that you are in touch with your inner voice, the next time you are upset, confused, or experiencing any negative emotions, ask your intuition to shed some light on the situation. I often will meditate when I need some quick answers to an upsetting situation. This helps me to get answers very quickly and to get rid of negative feelings. Having clarity about a situation can save you from many negative feelings.

Melissa was upset and angry because her co-worker, Ali, would often ignore her. During a session, I asked Melissa if she wanted to see what her intuition had to say about that situation. She emphatically agreed. As I guided Melissa through a meditation that helped her to tap into her own answers, she discovered that Ali's dislike toward her had nothing to do with her; it had everything to do with Ali's insecurity and jealousy. Melissa's intuition reminded her not to take things so personally. After Melissa got in touch with her intuition, she said to me with a big smile on her face: "I feel so much better." Your intuition can help you each and every day, if you allow it.

When I develop my intuition to the point where I receive total guidance, then:

_____

_____

_____

_____

Now that you have completed the seven-day exercise, why not turn up the volume on your intuition even more? This quick meditation will help you to access that place within yourself, at any time.

Special Place-Within Meditation

When you are ready, slowly take three deep breaths in through your nose and out through your mouth. After each exhale, you will become more relaxed. Gently close your eyes and see a door in front of you. Open the door and begin to slowly float down to that special place within yourself. As you float, you are letting go of everything that has been stopping you from being in a perfect state of peace. It feels so good to let go. Keep letting go. You are now at the bottom floor. Walk toward the large door that is in front of you. Open the door and enter that special place within where you have all your answers. You feel peaceful as you enter this place. Look around the room and stay focused on the beauty all around you. Begin to sit on the cozy chair that is in front of you. You are completely safe and relaxed. Now that you are feeling so safe and relaxed, ask your first question. Sit quietly in this room, as you patiently wait to hear the answer to your first question.

When you have received your answer, ask another question. Keep asking your questions, one at a time. Once you receive all your answers, you are going to walk back through the door and float back up to the top floor. There is a white light shining brightly on you as you continue to float. You feel great peace and joy.

Once you are on the top floor, you are going to slowly start to come back in the room. Feel your feet on the floor. Hear any noises that are around you. Take a deep breath in through your nose and out through your mouth. Gently open your eyes. Take a few minutes to write about the intuitive information you received, so that you can refer to this information at another time.

The intuitive information that I received was:

_____
_____
_____
_____

How did it feel to get in touch with your inner voice?

_____
_____
_____
_____

What new insight did you gain from doing this exercise? When I got in touch with my inner voice, I realized that:

_____
_____
_____
_____

Listening to your inner voice is very powerful. Once you master this, you no longer have to doubt yourself and be persuaded by others. Keep in mind that only good can come from listening to your intuition and trusting this precious gift that you were given!

"Often you have to rely on intuition."
— Bill Gates

Here is a writing exercise that will also help you access that special place within.

Writing Exercise for Accessing Your Intuition

Before you begin writing, you are going to access your inner voice. To begin this process, allow yourself to completely relax where you are sitting. Close your eyes and take three deep breaths in through your nose and slowly exhale through your mouth. See any stress, feelings, or situations that have been stopping you from being in a perfect state of peace melt away. Notice little ice cubes of feelings and situations begin to melt all around you. There is now a puddle of feelings and situations that have melted on the ground near your feet. You are now completely free from all negative feelings and situations.

Take another deep breath in through your nose and slowly exhale through your mouth. Now that you have gotten rid of any feelings and situations that have been stopping you from being in a perfect state of peace, see a big white light surrounding your body. Breathe this white light into your body. See the light become even brighter around your stomach. As the white light surrounds this area of your body, your intuition is beginning to open like a lotus flower. See your intuition begin to fully awaken inside of you. Stay focused on the white light in your stomach.

Now that you have fully accessed your intuition, take another deep breath in through your nose and slowly exhale through your mouth. Open your eyes and begin writing on a sheet of paper, "Thank you, intuition, for your guidance." You are then going to write, "What do I need to know at this moment?" Allow your intuition to speak through your pen. Keep writing until the page you are writing on is completely covered. Do not judge the information that you receive, just keep writing as fast as you can. After you are done writing, take another deep breath in through your nose and slowly exhale through your mouth. The more you do this exercise, the more you will be getting in touch with your intuition.

This writing exercise helped me to see:

_____

_____

_____

Keep doing the exercises in this chapter over and over until they become a natural part of your life. The more I did these exercises, the more my intuition quickly and clearly spoke to me. The time and effort that you put into developing your intuition will be completely worth it. Let your intuition guide you to the beautiful life you deserve!

CHAPTER 9

How to Be in Your Power

*"The most common way people give
up their power is by
thinking they don't have any."*
— *Alice Walker*

Being in your power means listening to your intuition, following your intuition, trusting yourself, and standing up for yourself, without allowing anyone to convince you that what you are thinking, feeling, or doing is wrong. When you are fully in your power, not only will you feel internally strong, but no one will be able to take advantage of you. You will take great care of yourself in any given situation, regardless of how others respond. You will also stand firm on what you believe is right. True happiness comes when you are in your power! As you heal, support yourself with taking one step each day to be in your power.

After surviving a very abusive childhood, filled with despair, I had to do a lot of hard work to develop being in my power. For many years of my life, it was difficult for me to stand up for myself and not allow others to control or take advantage of me. Before I mastered being in my power, I attracted men who were emotionally unhealthy. I was often deeply hurt if someone responded to me in a harsh way. Not being in my power caused me inner turmoil. The more I put the tools, techniques, and information provided throughout this chapter into practice, the more I developed my power and began to live a life of peace, joy, and freedom. I also attracted a wonderful, healthy man who has added to my life.

When you are in your power, you will no longer make excuses for not fulfilling your heart's desires. For some, their heart's desire may be to positively impact people's lives. For others, it may mean fully developing their talents. When you are in your power, you will be unstoppable in fulfilling what is in your heart, regardless of any obstacles or any negative feedback that you may receive. You will not just wish or hope for something to happen; you will take all the necessary steps to make what is in your heart a reality. If it is not for your highest good for something to happen, then you will quickly move forward and know that what you just went through was a step you needed to take in order to make what is truly in your heart a reality.

You may have something in your heart, but you are resisting it because you want things to be done your way. When you trust your intuition, you will see that your life is being perfectly guided, even when you do not get exactly what you had hoped. When you are in your power, you will give up the useless battle of making what you want happen if it is not for your highest good. Great freedom comes when you are fully in your power. It will be easy for you to take excellent care of yourself and set clear boundaries. Standing up for yourself and for others will be automatic. Accepting manipulation or any form of mistreatment will be a thing of the past. Your people-pleasing days will be over. Feeling obligated to do things for others because you think you "should" will no longer happen. Saying "no" to the things that you do not want to do or are not right for you will be second nature.

Believing in yourself will be a natural part of life, regardless of whether or not anyone believes in you. You will make decisions that add to your life, not send you spiraling down an emotional hole. Most important, when you are in your power, you will rely on your inner voice to guide you. You will no longer doubt yourself or your intuition. You will support what you intuitively know you need to do or say in any given situation. Therefore, you will be well on your way toward creating a happy, peaceful life.

> *"When I discover who I am, I'll be free."*
> *— Ralph Ellison*

When I am fully in my power, my life will be different because:

_____

_____

_____

_____

Whenever you are going through a severe crisis, trauma, or loss and you have not mastered being in your power, it is not uncommon to go in and out of your power. On the days when you feel strong and good, you are more likely to be in your power. When you begin to doubt yourself and become negative in your thoughts and actions, you will temporarily suppress your inner power. Be gentle and patient with yourself during this difficult time. Once you are in your power, no one will be able to turn off your internal power light switch. At that point, your confidence in yourself and trust will keep that switch on at all times.

You may be thinking that you do not know where to begin with getting in touch with your inner power. You can begin by listening to your intuition, which will help you to access your inner power. Now think of a time when you had a strong negative response when someone asked you to do something. That was your inner voice speaking to you. Perhaps you heard that voice say, "No, no, this is not right for me." Yet, you politely said, "Oh sure, that would be fine." After those words came out of your mouth, you felt something was not right. You may have had a physical reaction that came from ignoring what was right for you. Perhaps you felt a knot in your stomach as you went into the people-pleasing mode. Not only did you ignore your inner voice, but you also suppressed your inner power.

I know that I have had this experience many times in my life. Now that I am in my power, this no longer happens. Being in your power creates a calm feeling unlike anything you have ever experienced. Take a few minutes to think about someone you know who is not in their power. I bet that person has a significant amount of drama in his or her life.

You cannot fully listen and follow your intuition, nor be in your power, if you are not taking good care of yourself. You are doing yourself a great disservice by putting your needs on hold for other people. When you stop putting your happiness in the gutter, you will instantly feel better.

As you slowly begin to listen to your inner voice, take good care of yourself, and be in your power, other people are not going to like that you have changed. Their dislike of how you have changed is generally because you are no longer catering to their needs. Your positive changes will mean a loss to them. I cannot tell you how many of my patients have said to me, "You were right; people do not like that I am no longer pleasing them and that I am in my power." Do not step back into the people-pleasing mode because you are uncomfortable that others are not happy about the way you have changed. In time, they will slowly start to adjust to your new way of being. During this time of transition, it is best to rely on any healthy support that you have. If you do not have anyone in your life who is able to support you with being in your power, then join a group in your community where people are likely to support you. It is very important to have support so that you can be solidly rooted in being in your power.

When Julie started seeing me for counseling, she was in the ugly habit of pleasing everyone. She knew that she was not in her power. Her life was a total mess. Her parents controlled her life in every way possible. During the first few months of our work together, I helped her to recognize how she gave her power away. Julie said that she wanted to be in her power but that it was just too difficult for her since her parents were overbearing.

Slowly, Julie started to listen to her intuition and be in her power. After Julie started her new job, she wanted to take a break from counseling. At that point, Julie was not deeply rooted in her power. Being in her power was new for her. Months later, I got a call from Julie. She wanted to see me immediately because she was experiencing great emotional distress for once again not being in her power. When she sat in my office, she said, "Once I stopped seeing you, I stopped being in my power and everything is a mess." What happened was that Julie needed more time, practice, and support to be solidly rooted in her power.

Being in your power also means being able to ask for what you need, which includes asking for help. Throughout most of my life, I thought that I had to do everything on my own. I never considered asking anyone for help. This made my life more difficult than it needed to be. When I learned years ago that a healthy person is someone who can ask for help when they need it, I slowly started asking for help. At first, this was uncomfortable for me. However, once I reaped the rewards of asking for help, I allowed myself to work through the temporary discomfort. Several years ago, I wanted to move my baby grand piano out of my living room and into an empty room that had recently been painted. Instead of spending hundreds of dollars to hire movers, I asked three friends who happened to stop by if they could lend a hand. Within fifteen minutes, my piano was moved. My friends were happy to help me and I was happy to receive their help. In the past, I never would have dared ask for such help. I would have told myself that I would be inconveniencing my friends and that I just needed to hire the movers. This is nonsense!

How often do you ask for help when you need it? What do you believe about asking for help? Do you feel that you would be inconveniencing someone if you asked for their help? You are not alone. Many people feel that way. What beliefs stop you from asking for help? The truth is that most people feel great when helping others. We are not meant to accomplish great things on our own. In fact, most people who have accomplished anything worthwhile have had much help along the way.

You are fooling yourself if you believe that you have to do things completely on your own. Perhaps some past disappointments created this belief. When you do not ask for help, you are cheating people out of the opportunity to feel great about contributing to your life. Perhaps another reason why you have trouble asking for help is because you see it as a sign of weakness. There is nothing weak about asking for help. Your life does not need to be extra hard by doing everything on your own. Break free from the limiting belief that you have to do everything on your own and allow people to help you! When you accept the help you need, you will have more time to focus on being in your power.

Strengthening Your Inner Power

Here is a list of things you can do each day. The more you do these things on the list, the more you will be strengthening your inner power.

- Listening to my intuition.
- Honoring my intuition.
- Saying "no" when I need to.
- Standing up for myself when someone tries to take advantage of me.
- No longer allowing anyone to use me.

- No longer pleasing others at my expense.
- Thinking positively.
- Speaking kindly to my adult self and my inner child.
- Being happy.
- Feeling good.
- Listening to music, watching a movie, reading a book that uplifts my spirit.
- Not caring what others think.
- Being a best friend to myself at all times.
- Making plans that work for me.
- Taking consistent, massive action in my life.
- Resolving what I can immediately.
- Giving to others, while setting limits to how much I give.
- Allowing nature to nurture me.
- Having relationships that add to my life.
- Surrounding myself with people who are supportive of me.
- No longer accepting any form of mistreatment.
- Doing what I feel is best for me.
- Expressing my thoughts/feelings.
- Taking great care of my body, mind, and spirit.
- Nurturing myself.
- Treating myself well.
- Being authentic.
- Acquiring knowledge.

- Feeling my feelings.
- Pursuing my heart's desires.
- Doing things that I enjoy.
- De-stressing every day.
- Eating well.
- Getting enough rest.
- Exercising.
- Experiencing lots of joy.
- Asserting myself when something does not feel right.
- Asserting myself when I want or need something.
- Removing myself from unhealthy situations.
- Making good choices.
- Putting myself in situations that feel good.
- Surrounding myself with people who see the good in me.
- Standing up for what I believe is right.
- Not allowing anyone to control or mistreat me in any way.
- Ending conversations that do not feel right to me.
- Asking for help when I need it.
- Becoming fully aware of my needs and meeting those needs.
- Making choices that I know are right for me, regardless of what others think.
- Loving myself.
- Developing my spirituality.
- Meditating.

- Being kind and loving to everyone.
- Trusting myself.
- Letting go when things are out of my control.
- Fully relying on my intuition.
- Trusting Life.

> *"A man cannot be comfortable without his own approval."*
> — *Mark Twain*

Other things I can do to be in my power are:

_____

_____

_____

_____

_____

How many of these things on the list do you do each day? What has stopped you from doing these things?

_____

_____

_____

I am now ready to be in my power because:

_____

_____

_____

Now that you are ready to be in your power, set yourself up for success. Each day, do at least one thing that helps you to move toward being in your power. Gradually increase the number of things that you do on the list. If you are ready to do more than one thing each day from the list, then go for it! However, do not overwhelm yourself with doing too much at once. Be patient with yourself. If you push yourself too much, you will get discouraged. Keep taking baby steps toward the goal of being in your power. These baby steps make all the difference in the world. In time, you will be amazed at how you are automatically doing the things on this list.

When I first started counseling Sofia, she was used to being disempowered. People at work took advantage of her. Her husband and children took advantage of her. She often felt like an invisible child who was stuck in an adult body. Sofia was taught as a little girl that she had to please everyone and keep her mouth shut at all times. She believed that it was wrong to ever have any needs, wants, or desires. Asserting herself was out of the question. She lived a very lonely, unhappy life for many years. Not only did Sofia have some childhood healing to do, but she also needed to learn how to listen to her inner voice and be in her power.

As Sofia began to learn in counseling what her needs were, the next step was for her to begin to meet those needs. As she slowly started to learn to take care of herself and meet her needs, she started to listen to her intuition. As Sofia started to listen to her intuition, I helped her to slowly be in her power. At first, this terrified her. She wavered between enjoying being in her power and continuing to struggle with her childhood beliefs that she was supposed to be invisible and not heard, at which times she felt powerless. Once you are in your power, there is no such thing as being invisible and having no rights or a voice. As Sofia continued to work through her feelings and negative beliefs, she was able to keep on track more easily and remain in her power.

It took Sofia much work and healing to be in her power; however, today she is fully in her power and enjoying her life. She now has more peace than she ever dreamed she would experience in her life. People at work no longer take advantage of her. In fact, she is now receiving accolades that she has never heard from her boss in thirty years! Her husband and children no longer take advantage of her. She now takes great care of her body, mind, and spirit. Sofia is aware that being in her power has completely changed her life for the better.

Take Action to Be in Your Power

For the next seven days, keep track of what you are doing to be in your power. The more you focus on being in your power, the more you will blossom in this area.

Day 1. Today, the action that I took in order to be in my power was:

_____

_____

Day 2. What I did today to develop being in my power was:

_____

_____

Day 3. I focused on being in my power by:

_____

_____

Day 4. I allowed myself to strengthen my inner power by:

_____

_____

Day 5. I am now allowing myself to develop my inner power by:

_____

_____

Day 6. I can see that strengthening my inner power helps me to:

_____

_____

Day 7. I am now developing my inner power by:

_____

_____

You owe it to yourself to create a life of peace, joy, and happiness. Being in your power will help you achieve this life. When people are not in their power, they often experience turmoil, drama, and joylessness. Even though it may take a while for you to be fully in your power, keep working toward this goal every day. You will get there! Once you are in your power, your life will never be the same.

PART IV

Making Enjoyable Connections

CHAPTER 10

How to Develop Satisfying Relationships

Humans were created to be social. Relationships are meant to enhance and add to your life. Unfortunately, a great majority of people have experienced being drained by at least one person in their life. I have experienced this as well. An emotionally draining person may wish for you to throw them an emotional life raft, so that they can be saved from the tidal waves called "their feelings." These people would do everyone a great service if they took full responsibility for their life and healed their wounds. Even though they may be well intentioned, they can also be toxic. If someone in your life is emotionally wounded and not willing to heal, then they stand a good chance of being emotionally draining. Who drains you or has drained you? Which of your relationships adds stress to your life? If you feel stressed, drained, or unhappy, then there is room for growth.

Dysfunctional relationships can add much stress to your life. Whenever someone tries to control, manipulate, make you feel wrong, or hurt you in any way, you will surely experience stress and this does not feel good. This is a clear sign that your relationship is in need of repair. The converse is also true: healthy relationships will add joy to your life and help you feel good about yourself. As you heal, allow yourself to connect more with people who are supportive of you. This will help you.

"Your friends are God's way of apologizing for your relatives!"
— *Wayne W. Dyer*

When you allow someone to drain you, then you are contributing to their unhealthiness. It is possible to have a relationship with that person that feels good, but first you need to set very clear boundaries. You can do this by saying "no" to any requests they make of you that do not feel right, or by seeing them less frequently. These people will be uncomfortable when you start setting boundaries. You are clearly letting them know that your relationship with them has to change, and that it is not your job to take care of them emotionally. You are also letting them know that you are no longer going to accept mistreatment from them.

Being a people-pleaser will be a thing of the past once you set solid boundaries. Being a giving, loving person is great, but this should not be at your expense and make you feel lousy. You do not need to feel guilty about taking care of yourself. Whenever someone asks you an inappropriate question, you have the right to set a boundary there as well. This is healthy to do. Whenever someone crosses your boundaries by saying or doing something inappropriate, your body will react to this. Some of these reactions may include feeling angry, upset, or as though you have a knot in your stomach. Whenever your body has a strong reaction, ask yourself, "How can I take care of myself in this situation?" When someone asks you a question that does not feel right, you may want to say, "I do not want to talk about that" or "I want to keep that to myself." You have a right to take care of yourself in every situation! If you walk away from someone feeling emotionally drained, then you are pleasing that person at your expense.

There will be times when you enjoy being with an emotionally draining person. Take a few minutes to think of the times when being with this person has been good.

When you enjoyed spending time with that potentially draining person, what were you doing?

_____
_____

How much time did you spend together?

_____

What happened to make your time with that person good?

_____
_____

What did you do or say that helped you not feel drained?

_____
_____

Based on what you wrote, you now have some insight into what works for you. Why not continue to meet that person under those circumstances? This will help you to feel good, as you stay connected with that person.

You can test the boundaries every so often to see if you feel comfortable expanding the relationship by spending more time with him or her. If you allow yourself to be negatively impacted by anyone, then you are back to accepting mistreatment. Being drained is negative. Nothing good comes from this.

If you no longer accept negativity, not only will you feel better, but you will also have more energy. The more energy you have, the more you can create what you want. Give yourself the gift of spending time with people who add to your life. As you distance yourself from people's emotional webs, you will have more freedom to cultivate healthier relationships.

For years, I allowed myself to have relationships that completely drained my energy and took away from my happiness and good feelings about myself. I tried to get emotionally handicapped people to love me. I kept giving and giving to these people, while getting nothing in return. I could not understand why I was not getting back an ounce of what I gave. I figured that perhaps if I gave even more, then I would begin to get something back. I was wrong! The more I gave, the more hurt and empty I felt and the more they expected from me. I slowly realized that I really needed to give most of that good stuff to myself and to people who appreciated me. It took me a long time to understand that I did not have to have relationships that were unhealthy and dissatisfying. Today, I only have relationships that add to my life. Unfortunately, I had to let go of some relationships that were unhealthy and not going to change, no matter what I tried. You cannot change someone else. You can only change yourself. As a result of setting good boundaries, I no longer feel dissatisfied or unhappy in any of my relationships.

I still have a couple of people in my life who could possibly drain me if I allowed them. However, I set very clear boundaries so that they do not have the opportunity to take away from my happiness. It took me many years to discover that you can have a nice relationship with someone who is emotionally unhealthy. The key is to creatively figure out a way to make that happen. You may need to simply meet a potentially draining person for coffee, rather than spend an exorbitant amount of time with them. Perhaps taking a nice walk for an hour or meeting for a quick dinner will work.

There is nothing wrong with spending different amounts of time with each person in your life. Setting the boundary of limiting the amount of time with someone who is potentially draining can save you from much turmoil. If you feel good being around someone, and the relationship is healthy, then you may want to spend more time with that person. By limiting your contact with certain people, you are not abandoning them. You are just creating a healthier relationship with them. When you know how to fully take care of yourself, you will be much more relaxed and pleasant to be around. Even though emotionally unhealthy people may want to be around you often, they will benefit by you being relaxed and peaceful when they do see you.

Victoria was often giving to everyone. She felt "exhausted and suffocated" by the number of needy people in her life. Victoria realized that most of her relationships needed to change in order for her no longer to feel depleted. She slowly started to set boundaries. When Victoria first started to say no, her family, friends, and co-workers were irritated and uncomfortable with her new assertiveness. They tried very hard to get Victoria to be her old self by manipulating her. Several people told her that they were not happy with how she had changed and that she was now being selfish. What they really did not like was that she was no longer catering to their needs and giving up a part of herself to please them.

At first, Victoria struggled with everyone's disapproval. I informed her that when someone breaks an old pattern, everyone in that person's life may resist the change. Everyone in Victoria's life struggled with her no longer putting their needs first. Initially, everyone resented her new inner strength because this meant that they were losing all the good stuff that she gave them. Now when Victoria's family, friends, and co-workers try to manipulate her into doing what they want her to do, she will instantly stop the manipulation by saying, "No, that will not work for me, but thanks anyway."

If Victoria starts to feel drained, all she needs to do is change the conversation or politely excuse herself. Victoria now feels better than ever! She no longer faces a great deal of stress from putting everyone's needs first and from allowing people to drain her. By saying "no" to the things she does not want to do, she has more time to be good and loving toward herself. Not only does she feel great from no longer sacrificing herself to please others, but her relationships are more satisfying than ever. As a result of her new assertiveness, people are responding to her in a way that makes Victoria feel good, rather than "used." When her mother offered to cook Thanksgiving dinner for the first time since she got married more than twenty years ago, Victoria nearly fell out of her chair. In the past, her family assumed that Victoria was going to do this. Victoria is enjoying living a more balanced life as a result of her new assertiveness.

For many years, Marlene thought that she had to answer people's questions, regardless of what they were asking or how terrible she felt talking about something she did not want to talk about. Marlene thought that in order to be labeled as a very nice person, she had to please people no matter how much turmoil she felt. Through counseling, she learned that she had the right to set boundaries by only answering questions that she felt comfortable answering. Now that she sets very clear boundaries, she no longer experiences turmoil by violating her level of comfort. As you get in the habit of taking care of yourself, you too will have to say good-bye to much discomfort and turmoil.

Take a few minutes to look at all your relationships. Which people in your life drain you? Which people contribute to your feeling bad about yourself?

I feel drained or negatively impacted by:

1. _____
2. _____
3. _____

How to Develop Satisfying Relationships

In order for me to feel less drained and negatively impacted by _____, I need to:

_____

_____

_____

In order for me to feel less drained and negatively impacted by _____, I need to:

_____

_____

_____

In order for me to feel less drained and negatively impacted by _____, I need to:

_____

_____

_____

The people who make me feel bad about myself are:

1. _____
2. _____
3. _____
4. _____
5. _____

Now let us focus on the relationships that add to your life. It is important to have relationships that support your personal growth and help you feel good about yourself. Which people in your life support your personal growth and help you feel good about yourself? Who adds to your life? How do these people add to your life?

The people who add to my life are:
1._____
2._____
3._____
4._____
5._____

Each of these people add to my life by:

_____

_____

_____

_____

What new insight did you gain from doing this exercise?

The new insight that I gained from doing this exercise is:

_____

_____

_____

_____

Is there anything you can do to make your good relationships even better? Do you need to spend more time nurturing those relationships? Is it hard to admit that you are wrong at times? How effectively do you communicate with your family and friends? Good communication is essential in order for any relationship to be good. Do you keep loved ones at a distance by making assumptions? I find that many of the people I have counseled over the years create much distance in their relationships by doing this. Assumptions will block one of the most necessary ingredients to any good relationship: communication. This will often create drama and turmoil. When do you assume things? If you are unsure about something, then go to the proper source and ask questions. Get the information you need, so that you no longer play this toxic game.

It is also important to communicate what you are thinking and feeling. If you are not good at expressing your feelings and asking questions, then simply practice until you can do this easily. We all need to work on this at some point in our lives. When we are not good at communicating, this not only puts a damper on our relationships but it also stifles our ability to express who we are. Miscommunication often leads to resentment.

Even though it is important to have good, healthy relationships, that will not be possible if you do not have a good relationship with yourself. If you do not like being around you, then it will be difficult for others to enjoy being around you. No matter what, you can never get away from yourself. You will always be there wherever you go. What is your relationship with yourself like? Do you enjoy your own company at all times? Are you comfortable spending a solid day by yourself? Are you able to spend a few days alone and have a good time? The more you like and love yourself, the more people will want to be around you! How can you have a better relationship with yourself?

I can have a better relationship with myself by:

_____

_____

_____

_____

"No one can ask another to be healed. But he can let himself be healed, and thus offer the other what he has received. Who can bestow upon another what he does not have? And who can share what he denies himself?"
— *A Course in Miracles*

The only person in this world who can make your relationship with yourself good is YOU! If you have people in your life who are willing to have a good relationship with you, and these relationships will add to your life, then do your part. The rewards that come from developing these relationships will certainly be worth all your efforts! The better your relationships are, the happier you will be!

CHAPTER 11

How to Be a Giving Person

"We make a living by what we get,
but we make a life by what we give."
— *Norman MacEwen*

My mother is a giving, kind, and loving person to strangers. She will strike up a conversation with anyone. She has been a great role model by teaching me how to be a giving person and to cultivate relationships with people from all walks of life. When I was five years old, my mother asked me to gather all my Barbie dolls that I was willing to give to a poor family in the neighborhood. After I happily put my dolls in a box, Mom and I walked down the street to the family's house. I remember standing several feet behind my mother as she rang the doorbell. A kind woman with dark hair opened the door. My mother talked to her. I noticed that my mother's kindness left this woman beaming with joy. At that moment, Mom taught me how wonderful it is to give and how great it feels to open your heart to others, even strangers.

My mother has continued throughout my life to be one of the nicest, friendliest women I have ever known to everyone she meets. During my childhood, I vividly remember Mom offering kind words to a neighbor that everyone dismissed because she was very eccentric-looking. Again, Mom modeled to me how to be kind and loving to everyone.

Today, I have a wonderful group of friends from all different races and backgrounds. My life has been fully enriched by these incredible people. I have even had naive people say to me, "I would never have pictured you with the friends you have." Comments like this show me how closed-minded people can be. I could have been like some people, not open to all of life's good. Thanks to my mother, this was not an option for me. How open are you to receiving all of life's good? Are you going to judge people or are you going to be a giving person who can see the beauty in others' hearts? You can be closed-minded and live your life as a spiritually handicapped person or you can be open to all of life's good. The choice is yours!

The more you give, without being drained, the more your heart will dance with joy. There are countless ways to do this. A simple smile may brighten someone's day. Being thoughtful can touch a person's heart. Helping someone can transform their life. How are you a giving person? How can you be even more giving? You do not need to be rich to be a giving, kind person who makes a difference in this world. You can simply hold a door open for someone. Little acts of kindness have the power to impact people greatly, especially when they come from the heart. Do you take action and make what is in your heart reality?

"You can't live a perfect day without doing something for someone who will never be able to repay you."

— John Wooden

How to Be a Giving Person

My kind, dear acquaintance José has been working at Dunkin' Donuts for eight years. My routine at Dunkin' Donuts, at least a couple of times a week, is to grab a cup of coffee, and say "hi" to the staff. Throughout the years, every time I saw José, we would talk for a few minutes, as he stopped sweeping or mopping the floors. Most of that time he spoke only Spanish. Gradually he started to learn English. Now, eight years later, José speaks English very well.

I will never forget the magical moment when I went into Dunkin' Donuts after not having seen José for quite some time due to a change in his schedule and in mine. When I saw him, he was not mopping the floors or taking out the trash. He was standing behind the counter ready to ring up my coffee! As he did, I noticed that his name tag said MANAGER! I was in awe at that moment! I could not believe my eyes. I was so happy for José and so proud of him at the same time. If you had seen my reaction to his promotion, you would have thought I had just won the lottery!

I wanted to do something to acknowledge his promotion. I immediately went to a nearby chocolate store and bought José a smiley face container filled with gold chocolate stars. I then went back to Dunkin' Donuts and I gave him the small gift. I told José that I was very proud of him for being promoted. He told me that I was the only person who had acknowledged his promotion and that my gesture meant SO MUCH to him. I had no idea that my small acknowledgment would touch him the way it did. I simply followed what was in my heart. This is an example of how giving something small can touch someone's heart in a big way. José was so touched by my small gesture that he went out of his way to buy me a present to thank me for my support. Giving to others has enriched my life and given me much joy.

There is no reason why every person cannot give to others, especially since there are unlimited ways of giving. Saying something encouraging is an easy way to give, so is giving a compliment. How often do you say something encouraging to others or give compliments? People love to hear these things. This can forever impact someone's life. It most certainly will help to quickly change someone's state if they walk away feeling uplifted and good. How do you feel when someone encourages you or gives you a compliment that touches your heart? Of course you feel good.

Volunteering is a wonderful way to give. When was the last time you volunteered your time to help someone or make some type of positive change? This can be very healing, especially when you are going through a difficult time. A few years ago my friend Alyssa and I volunteered to help clean up an environment that was filled with garbage. I cannot tell you how much fun it was to transform that environment into a beautiful place. Alyssa said that she never knew that she could feel so good while picking up garbage! I enjoyed the whole experience, too. It was wonderful being able to take an environment that looked like a dumping ground and turn it into a beautiful place in less than five hours! How would you like to make a difference?

If you do not have time to volunteer at this point in your life, then why not find some wonderful charities and donate what you can? When you give to charities that speak to your heart, you will feel great giving what you can. Why not donate some of your used clothing or furniture? There are plenty of thrift shops that will sell your used goods and take those profits to directly help people and animals in your community. Your donations can make a big difference. When you give from your heart, not only will you be making a difference, but you will feel great in return.

"We must not only give what we have, we must give what we are."
— *Desire-Joseph Mercier*

Whenever I meet someone who is not a giving person, it is easy to see why they feel so empty on the inside. If only these people could open their hearts to others, then they would experience great inner joy that would fill their emptiness. Each of us has something to give to this world. There are many people who need what you have to offer. What talents have you been blessed with? If you have musical talent, why not share this gift with people who will be uplifted by hearing your talent in action? If you like to read, why not read to children, the elderly, the blind, or the sick? Give ….Give….Give…. and enjoy the wonderful feelings and experiences that automatically come from having a big heart!

"The place to improve the world is first in one's own heart and head and hands."
— *Robert M. Pirsig*

When you give, do not focus on what you will get back. This is not giving from the heart. Even though I give from my heart, my experiences have shown me that good things will happen to me in turn. A few months ago, I donated many bags of items to a local charity. I decided that I also wanted to get rid of an old desk that I no longer loved. Unfortunately, this desk had run its course and it was not in good enough condition to donate. After I threw the desk away, I envisioned the exact desk that I wanted. I had actually never seen the desk that I created in my mind, but I knew that I would eventually come across what I had envisioned.

Sure enough, I walked in a store and saw the desk that I envisioned up against a wall. I was both delighted and completely surprised to see that what I wanted was standing right in front of me! As soon as I saw it, I knew that it belonged to me. Well, so I thought. A woman in the store walked up to me and said, "Isn't that a great desk?" I told her that I loved it! She then said, "I put that desk on layaway." My breathing slowed down, to the point where I felt as though I was not breathing at all. The desk was not mine!

I could not believe what I had just heard. It did not make any sense to me. I thought for sure that it was mine. I was completely baffled. The woman then slowly said, "I put the desk on layaway; however, I decided a few minutes ago to take it off of layaway because the legs are a little wobbly." I immediately told the woman, with great excitement in my voice, that I loved it and that I was going to buy it. I then picked up the desk and carried it to the register. While I was waiting in line, three people walked up to me and told me that they really liked the desk. I knew that I was being blessed. By the way, it looks perfect in my den. I use it every day. I find that the more I give, the more I receive. Be a giving person and enjoy all the good that comes from it!

PART V

Rewarding Life's Actions

CHAPTER 12

Set Goals for Yourself

Working toward accomplishing a goal is a great way to get excited about life. When you let life take you by the wind, without any direction, you may end up constantly being thrown in a storm. If you are currently feeling difficult feelings, it would be beneficial to make small goals for yourself that will help your healing process. Each day, have the goal of taking a walk in nature for fifteen minutes. This will give you comfort and help you feel a little better. After you go for a walk, reward yourself. Perhaps you can buy your favorite coffee or tea on the way home or get yourself a small treat. Another goal that would be beneficial is to go out once a week with someone who is supportive of you. After you spend time with this person, reward yourself. As you begin to feel better, make new goals that will give you great pleasure once you achieve them.

As you heal, you will have moments of clarity. When that happens, ask yourself, "What do I want?" Do you want a new career or to start your own business? Do you want to take an art class? Would you like to go back to school and earn a degree? Do you want to be physically fit? Would you like to take that dream vacation? Would you like to volunteer? Do you want to be healed and happy, so that you can live an extraordinary life? After you get clear about what you want, write down this information in as much detail as possible. In order to create what you want, you need to make a commitment to do whatever it takes to accomplish your goals.

With hard work, talent, skill, and believing in yourself, you can accomplish what you want. However, this will not guarantee happiness. If you are emotionally unhappy as you work toward accomplishing your goals, then you will still be this way when you have what you want. There are some exceptions here. If you consciously choose to do internal work as you work toward accomplishing your goals, then you stand the chance of being happy even after you succeed.

Some people's lives look fantastic on the outside, yet they are miserable on the inside. Life is not only about what we create on the outside. More important, it is about the peace and joy that we create on the inside. The quality of your life cannot be good if you experience inner turmoil, even though you are accomplishing your goals. No one is exempt from doing internal work. When you go through a difficult experience, it is important to release any negative thoughts or feelings associated with that experience. By doing so, you are in the process of healing from that situation.

Your inner work will keep reappearing in your life until you give in and heal yourself on the inside. How many more crises do you need to experience before you are fully willing to heal your old and new wounds? You will do yourself a great service by making a commitment to heal, rather than continue to accumulate more turmoil. Yes, healing takes work and it can be frustrating at times. However, it is important to remember that working toward accomplishing ANYTHING worthwhile takes work. Creating inner peace after life throws curve balls at you takes work.

However, the rewards will be worth all your efforts. Becoming healed and creating lasting inner peace is no different from accomplishing other goals. You need to have a roadmap and take small steps toward achieving that goal. This book is your roadmap!

You cannot accomplish the goal of being peaceful and happy if you are carrying around all the emotional pain that you stuffed throughout your life. A healed person is free from the emotional ties of the past. If you are still emotionally connected to your past, then work toward pruning those roots. Take your inner shears and slowly clip away toward freedom. If your life is not peaceful and flowing easily, then you know that you have some internal work to do. There is nothing shameful about needing to heal. Most people are in need of emotional healing. When we are filled with emotional pain, the turmoil inside occupies our place of peace. Once you slowly remove that turmoil through healing, inner peace will reside within you.

When you have not healed, you will live a much more difficult life than the one that is intended for you. Having old stuff to heal is like having an old mildewy pond that follows you everywhere. Whenever life throws another rock at you, you get splashed with many past emotions that you never felt. Your job is to dry up this old pond by getting rid of the mildew one scoop of feelings and healing at a time. Once your pond no longer exists, life can continue to throw a rock at you, but you will no longer get splashed from the past. Your rock will simply hit the ground. There will no longer be a ripple effect. You will just have to deal with the current feelings that this new situation offers. Why not make one of your goals to be completely free from all forms of emotional turmoil? This will be one of the best goals you can possibly make for yourself!

Accomplishing anything worthwhile takes hard work! Most people cringe at this thought. If you want to lose those extra pounds, it will take commitment, hard work, and perseverance in order for you to succeed. Some people act as though accomplishing their goals were so easy. This is often not the case! Whenever you see someone with a great body, the chances are that they had to work incredibly hard to get that way. They certainly did not eat ice cream, chocolate, and potato chips every night before bed. They ate very well and exercised regularly.

One of my good friends said that she was ready to throw an object at her television while she was watching a drama that portrayed writing a book as such a simple task that could be done in a few days. This friend learned from me how much work is truly involved in writing a book. Even the media wants to portray accomplishing major goals as a simple task. This is unfortunate because then people get very frustrated when they face the reality of how much work they have to put into accomplishing some of their major goals.

As you work toward accomplishing what you want, yes, you may face many obstacles along the way. You need to keep moving forward even when you are not getting the results as fast as you want. The major difference between people who succeed and fail often has to do with perseverance. You may actually be more qualified to accomplish your goals than most people, but maybe you give up easily. Therefore, nothing comes to fruition. When the going gets rough, do you squash your goals and run in the opposite direction? That is a great way to create nothing but regrets that you can focus on when you are sitting on a rocking chair looking back on your life. I do not know about you, but I certainly do not want to have a list of regrets. Goals are meant to be accomplished, not put on the shelf because you do not feel like taking action.

In order to keep yourself motivated, you need to make sure that your goals excite you. They also need to be realistic and attainable. If you think that you can have a perfect body in six weeks after being fifty pounds overweight, you are setting yourself up for failure right from the beginning. It will take time to lose that weight. As with any success, it is a must to create an action plan that will clearly spell out the steps you need to take in order to accomplish your goals. If you discover that your plan is not giving you the results you want, then it may be time to tweak your plan.

Think about what beliefs and thoughts you will need to have in order to accomplish your goals. If you want to lose that extra weight, but you believe that you cannot do it because you love food too much, then you will do everything to sabotage your weight loss. Negative beliefs will stop you from achieving your goals. Is there anything in your life that you want, but for some reason it has not happened? Perhaps your limiting beliefs are holding you back. Be really honest with yourself as you examine your beliefs in the next exercise.

"If I have the belief that I can do it, I shall surely acquire the capacity to do it, even if I do not have it at the beginning."

— *Mahatma Gandhi*

Rhonda grew up in a home where her father's alcoholism and verbal abuse made her feel "unworthy and not good enough." And she had low self-esteem and the poor choices that go along with thinking that way. Rhonda's father would often tell her she was fat and not as pretty or smart as her sisters. Her negative beliefs had blocked her throughout her life, but it wasn't until her mother died in her early thirties that she realized it. In a moment of clarity, she understood that her childhood wounds had "always seemed to get in the way of me being happy" and that she needed to heal from these old wounds as well as the new ones. During a writing exercise called Change Your Beliefs, Rhonda was startled to realize how her negative beliefs were blocking her.

Once she identified those beliefs and saw that they weren't serving her, she was able to replace them with new beliefs and fill up with positive thoughts. I will never forget the last day I counseled Rhonda. Tears trickled down her face as she said, "I now feel good enough and worthy enough. I'm finally happy!"

Change Your Beliefs

What I really want is:

_____

_____

_____

_____

_____

My beliefs that are stopping me from having what I want are:

_____

_____

_____

_____

_____

_____

In order to have _____, I need to believe:

_____

_____

_____

_____

_____

Take a minute to review your limiting beliefs. You are now going to change those limiting beliefs and make them your new affirmations. If you believe that you are not smart enough to accomplish your goals, then your new affirmation is, "I am intelligent." If you believe that you are not talented enough to accomplish what you want, say to yourself, "Every day, I am seeing clearly how talented I am." You may be thinking that you cannot tell yourself these messages since you do not believe them. The more you repeat what you tell yourself, the more you will believe it. Post your affirmations on the mirror where you can read them often throughout your day.

My new affirmations are:
1._____
2._____
3._____

Positive Thinking

Not only do limiting beliefs have the ability to sabotage your goals, but negative thoughts also have that ability. You may believe that your goals are possible, but you tell yourself that you are selfish to even think about having what you want. By holding on to this one thought, you might as well throw your goals in the gutter. If you do take action while repeating this limiting thought, you will convince yourself that you do not want to be selfish, so forget about working toward what you want. In order to move forward on the right track, all your thoughts need to be positive. It is important to be your own cheerleader, regardless of whether or not anyone else is cheering you on along the way.

What supportive thoughts can you tell yourself that will motivate you as you work toward achieving your goals?

The thoughts that I am going to tell myself that will help me to achieve my goals are:

_____

_____

_____

_____

_____

Stay focused on the fact that you do not need to accomplish your goals overnight. Keep taking baby steps as you work toward achieving your desired outcomes. Before you take any action, think about how you are going to ultimately reward yourself for your success. Not only will small rewards along the way help to motivate you, but giving yourself a big reward once you accomplish your goals will also motivate you. When you focus on rewarding yourself, do you feel excited? If not, then think of another way you can reward yourself that really excites you. Take a few minutes to think about how great you are going to feel when you accomplish your goal. Hold on to these feelings for as long as you can. Now celebrate your successes in your mind. Do not let go of that experience just yet. Take in the excitement even more. Become aware of how your body feels now that you have accomplished this goal. Are you jumping up and down with excitement? See yourself running on the beach shouting, "I did it! Yes!" Whenever you experience frustration as you work toward accomplishing your goals, refer back to these feelings and the image of you celebrating your success. That image will help keep you motivated.

> *"Good thoughts are no better than good dreams,*
> *unless they be executed."*
> *— Ralph Waldo Emerson*

Now take a few minutes to think about how your life will be different when you achieve the goal of having total freedom in every area of your life. How will you feel? Take a few minutes to visualize yourself living this way. Stay focused on how great it feels. See yourself running on the beach with great joy from living the life you truly want.

It is important to fully celebrate each new freedom, which will help you to stay motivated as you work on this goal. You just started a new workout program. How are you going to celebrate your success with doing the program each month? You have just signed up for a class that you have been putting off for years. How are you going to celebrate? When you are out of debt, how are you going to celebrate? You have extra weight to lose. How are you going to celebrate when you lose that weight? You were wounded in childhood. How are you going to celebrate when you are free from the past? You are currently in the tunnel. How are you going to celebrate when you have made your way through it to the other side? Give as much detail as possible about how you are going to do this.

> *"A life filled with celebration is a rich one indeed."*
> — *Donald O. Clifton and Paula Nelson*

Take another minute to think about what you would like to be free from. Now focus on how you are going to celebrate that new freedom in your life.

The way that I am going to celebrate my new freedom of _____ is by:

_____

_____

_____

The way that I am going to celebrate my new freedom of _____ is by:

_____

_____

_____

The way that I am going to celebrate my new freedom of _____ is by:

_____

_____

_____

Now refer back to what you just wrote. Get in touch with the feelings that you will experience once you have total freedom in each of those areas of your life. Do you feel great joy, excitement, and happiness? How does it feel to celebrate? At this moment, hold on to the feelings even longer. The more you focus on this, the easier it will be to make this happen. As you create each new freedom, honor your original agreement to celebrate in these ways. If there are more ways that you can be free, continue with this exercise on another sheet of paper. Do not put off celebrating. If it takes you awhile to obtain each thing that you wrote, then so be it. Before you know it, you will have total freedom in all areas of your life! You now have something to look forward to. If you doubt that you will have this, stop telling yourself that lie! You are meant to have this and more; however, you need to do your part. In order to achieve freedom from within, you will need to heal, grow, give, spiritually evolve, and take excellent care of yourself.

Britney had deep debt, mostly from graduate school, which created much stress and turmoil in her life. This became a black cloud that followed her wherever she went. She believed that in the near future she *would be financially free, despite the fact that she owed over $100,000 on credit cards and at times barely had enough money to pay the minimum payments. Even though it looked as though Britney was never going to get out of debt, she knew in her heart that what seemed impossible was possible.*

It took Britney several years to get out of debt. Her faith and belief that she would one day be out of debt helped her turn her situation around. It gave her the courage, determination, and strength to take all the necessary steps in order for her to be financially free. Britney now feels great from this new freedom.

You too need to believe that you will have freedom in all areas of your life and do your part to make that happen. Keep holding on to this, even when things look bleak. You may be asking right now, "Why would I even think about freedom when I am in turmoil?" When you look beyond your temporary suffering, while believing that your future will be good, you are fully embracing this possibility. If you tell yourself that life is horrible now and it will continue to be nothing but horrible, then you are sinking in deeper mud. By believing that you will obtain freedom in every area of your life, this belief will catapult you powerfully toward making that happen. Enjoy your freedom!

CHAPTER 13

Follow Your Heart's Desires

Having a heart's desire is not the same as having goals that you want to work toward. You may have the goal of losing ten pounds so that you can fit into your old clothes. That is simply a goal of yours. Having a heart's desire has much more meaning. When you accomplish what is in your heart, you will be deeply fulfilled and satisfied. The joy that you experience from this will be worth all your hard work. Life is too short not to take action. None of us knows how long we will be here. Putting off your heart's desires can lead to having an unfulfilled, empty life, which will only create regrets. You have certain desires for a reason, which is to make them a reality.

Your heart may simply desire peace, or you may want to help eradicate hunger throughout the world. Only you know what is truly in your heart. You have everything within you to bring this to fruition. Do not let anyone hold you back from what is meant for your life. Accomplishing your heart's desires will make your heart sing with incredible joy!

For years, I felt a strong desire to give love and acceptance to children in need. I was fortunate to travel to India for two weeks, and had a magical experience when all forty or so children in one village started following me around. When I began to sing a few lines from a child's song in English, they did their best to sing it back. I spent several hours teaching the children over twenty children's songs in English as they laughed, skipped, and beamed with joy. When it was time for me to leave, they begged me to stay, hugging me tightly one by one. I felt so sad saying good-bye to them. Later our tour guide told me that he had been doing this for many years and had never seen those children respond so positively to anyone. Magic can happen when you carry out your heart's desires. It was an experience I will treasure forever!

> *"If you want happiness for an hour, take a nap.*
> *If you want happiness for a day,*
> *go fishing. If you want happiness for a year,*
> *inherit a fortune. If you want*
> *happiness for a lifetime, help somebody."*
> *— Chinese Proverb*

Your Heart's Desires

What is truly in your heart? Have you ever wanted to help people in need? Is it in your heart to volunteer, so that you could positively impact someone? Do you have a special talent that you have not focused on in years? Perhaps you have always wanted to travel to Italy. What has been stopping you from pursuing your heart's desires? Have you ever thought about how you would feel once you accomplish what is in your heart? I know firsthand that you will experience an incredible amount of joy!

I am passionate not only about making a difference in people's lives, but also about helping animals. I have always been a big animal lover. For a while, it was in my heart to give my local animal shelter some jewelry that I'd collected over the past fifteen years. I felt great knowing that I was going to be helping the animals by giving them those things to sell. As I was dropping off the items, I told one of the owners that I wanted the shelter to have some really good jewelry, for which I gave him a copy of an appraisal that I had. I was hoping that they would auction off one of the pieces of jewelry I gave them, so that they could make a nice profit that would help the animals.

The next week, I went back to the shelter so that I could donate some more things. As soon as I walked toward the shelter's thrift shop, a gentleman I had never seen before greeted me. I told him that I had some more jewelry and other things for the shelter. I also mentioned that I donated one particularly good piece of jewelry the week before. He immediately said to me with great excitement in his voice, "You are Campbell." I was so surprised. How did he know my last name? He proceeded to say that people were touched by what I had given the shelter the week before and that I had no idea what I had done for them. He also said that one of the women who worked for him purchased a bracelet that I gave them and that she was crying as she told him that she never owned anything so nice in her life. He mentioned that my donations were really going to help the shelter, especially since they were struggling.

As I walked in the thrift shop with that gentleman, carrying some of my donations, he firmly said in front of everyone, "Guess who this is?" Everyone looked clueless. He then said, "This is Campbell." One woman immediately ran over to me and said, "Oh my gosh, can I hug you?" After I gave her a hug, she said, "Thank you so much for the donations." The ten minutes that I spent that day at the SPCA completely touched my heart. I was awed by that experience. I had no idea that what I was donating would have so great an impact.

After I left the shelter, I parked my car outside a doughnut shop and cried because I felt so deeply touched by the experience. If I had not followed through with what was in my heart, I would have missed out on one of the most touching moments of my life.

Get Rid of Your Excuses

Is there something in your heart that you keep putting off? When you accomplish your heart's desires, you cannot help but feel great. You may be putting off what is in your heart because of the excuses that you make. I completely understand this. In the past, I had a list of excuses for not pursuing some of my heart's desires. This has caused me great pain and regret.

For years, it was in my heart to contact a dear co-worker of mine, Joanne, whom I lost contact with in 1994 after I moved. Joanne and I had a close relationship throughout the six years we worked together. She was always warm, caring, and supportive. Everyone loved Joanne. I dearly loved her. I still can see her clear as crystal in my mind. She always seemed to be laughing. As the years went by, I kept thinking that I needed to get in touch with Joanne. But I kept putting it off, making excuse after excuse for why it was not the right time for me to see her.

A few years ago, I decided that I had to push myself to see her. Shortly after my decision, I ran into another former co-worker who said that Joanne had recently passed away. I absolutely could not believe that this was true. I had missed the opportunity to see her all because of the excuses that I made. I will no longer make that mistake. This taught me never to put off my heart's desires. I never would have imagined that the one person I wanted to see more than anyone in the world was someone who had passed away.

Do not make the same mistake. I wish that someone would have told me years ago what I am telling you now. The biggest excuse that I made for not seeing Joanne when I had the chance was that I wanted to wait to see her when I was fully happy. Little did I know that my excuse was forever going to rob me of the chance of having my heart's desire.

You may have told yourself, "I will work toward my heart's desires in the future." When the future comes, you will say, "I should have done that when I was younger. Now I am too old to do that." Does this sound familiar? Your excuses will get you nowhere. Living a life of regrets is nothing to be proud of. It is better to have tried to pursue all your heart's desires than not try at all.

Are you ready to give up your excuses for not taking action toward having your heart's desires? If your answer is yes, Good For You! For now, take a few minutes to quietly think about your heart's desires. Have you always wanted to visit an old friend? Is there a family member you need to patch things up with? Have you ever wanted to sing in a choir? Later in this chapter, you will be asked to write about your heart's desires and come up with a plan for accomplishing them. For now, just stay focused on tuning in to some of them.

Make a commitment to pursue your heart's desires, regardless of any obstacles that you face. Is it in your heart to go back to school? Have you ever wanted to open your own business? Do you want to write a book? Have you always wanted to make a career out of the one thing that you are most passionate about? Do you want to try something new? You will not know if you enjoy doing something until you give it a try. What did you enjoy doing when you were younger? People often go through life without asking themselves these questions. They just go along with the flow of life, even if they feel only half alive. When you accomplish your heart's desires and love what you are doing, you will have a renewed passion for life. When do you feel fully alive?

I feel fully alive when:

_____

_____

_____

_____

When you feel fully alive, you are fulfilling some of your heart's desires. Why not make these things a bigger part of your life? If you were living your heart's desires and someone stopped you from doing this, guess what would happen? You guessed it. You would be angry and unhappy;

therefore, your life would be passionless, dull, and boring. That would not be acceptable to you. Yet, you are the one who is stopping yourself from living that kind of life and you tell yourself that it is okay to live that way. You say, "Well, this is how most people live." Your desires were not put in your heart for you to ignore them and feel half alive. Your desires are there for you to experience all the joy that comes from having them.

We live in a world of unlimited possibilities and yet very few people venture out in the world and experience some of these possibilities. Your life will completely change when you overcome your fear and give yourself permission to do so. How has fear stopped you from making your heart's desires come to fruition? Do you tell yourself that it is easier to live a mediocre life than to take risks? You are not alone! There are many people who become dreamers, without taking action. They simply move through life secretly wishing they had pursued their dreams.

"You gain strength, courage and confidence
by every experience in which you
really stop to look fear in the face."
— *Eleanor Roosevelt*

Holding on to fear will only support your excuses for not taking action. *That is what happened to Rick. For many years, he longed to start a Web site business, but he was always full of excuses for why it would be impossible. Being laid off from the corporation where he had worked for nineteen years may have been the perfect opportunity to pursue his dream, but he convinced himself that he needed another stable job. Rick sent out hundreds of resumes and went on several interviews over the course of two years, but received no job offers. When his savings were completely wiped out, his credit card nearly maxed out, and his marriage on the brink of divorce, Rick felt he was headed toward a nervous breakdown. Out of desperation, he finally opened his own business—and it took off. Rick would have saved himself much debt and turmoil if he had taken this step sooner.*

Are you like Rick? Do you let fear stop you? Why not feel the fear and continue to take action?

Writing Exercise: Accomplishing Your Heart's Desires

Take a few minutes to get clear about what is in your heart.

It is in my heart to:

_____

_____

_____

_____

Now take those things that you just wrote and put them on a big piece of paper where you can see them every day. This list will motivate you to take action and have what was intended for your life. Tucking that list away where you cannot see it will only support your excuses.

Achieving your heart's desires very often takes work. Most people cringe at this thought. If you want to open your own business, it will take hard work, a commitment, and perseverance in order for you to succeed. As with accomplishing goals, some people make having their heart's desires look easy, so we think that it should be easy for us to achieve the same. In most cases, that is not true! Look at Olympic athletes— they make everything look so easy and yet they work unbelievably hard. Their whole lives revolve around their heart's desire of winning a gold medal. When you were younger you may have fantasized about being in the Olympics, without having any clue about what it would take to get there. As an adult, it is easy to be in awe when you think about how incredibly hard each athlete has worked to achieve this dream.

As you work toward accomplishing your heart's desires, you may encounter many bumps in the road, whether you want to change careers, go back to school, or write a book. Of course, if it is your heart's desire to do something like travel to Europe, this will be different. You will need to research where you would like to travel, put aside the funds, book your trip, get your passport, pack your suitcase, and enjoy the experience. However, most heart's desires take harder work. As long as you have a plan that you know will help you to achieve your heart's desires, keep moving forward one step at a time. Your heart's desires are meant to come to fruition!

Have you ever spoken to someone who has achieved what is in your heart? This is a great way to discover what action you need to take and what obstacles you are likely to face. Having a realistic perspective on what you can expect will provide you with valuable information. Are you like most people, giving up because you are not getting results fast enough? How willing are you to keep moving forward even when it looks like nothing is happening? Once you take action toward accomplishing what is in your heart, do not give up out of frustration. This is likely to occur, but do not let it discourage you. When you hit some bumps in the road, take a break, and then move forward.

In order to keep yourself motivated, you need to make sure that you continue to focus on making your heart's desires come to life. As with goals, it is essential to have a roadmap that clearly spells out all the action steps you need to take in order to accomplish what is in your heart. If you discover that your roadmap is not producing results, it may be time to tweak your action steps.

"Man is what he believes."
— Anton Chekhov

Now that you know what is in your heart, what beliefs and thoughts will support you in achieving it? If you want to start your own business, but you believe that you will not be successful, then this limiting belief will sabotage your success. Negative beliefs have the power to destroy your heart's desires. The reverse is also true. Positive beliefs will continue to recharge your spirit as you move through frustration.

Change Your Beliefs

My beliefs that are stopping me from achieving my heart's desires are:

_____
_____
_____
_____

In order to accomplish my heart's desires, I need to believe:

_____
_____
_____
_____

Now that you have identified which beliefs will support you in achieving what is in your heart, make these your new affirmations. If you believe that you are not worthy enough to have what is in your heart, your new affirmation will be, "I am more than worthy of having what is in my heart." If you believe that you are not capable of accomplishing your heart's desires, say to yourself, "I am more than capable of accomplishing my heart's desires." Post your new affirmations where you can read them every day. It does not matter that you do not believe your new affirmations at this moment. When you repeat them enough, you will start to believe them. This will help you move in the direction of accomplishing your heart's desires.

My new affirmations are:

1._____
2._____
3._____

"Everyone has inside of him a piece of good news. The good news is that you don't know how great you can be! How much you can love! What you can accomplish! And what your potential is."

—*Anne Frank*

Ellen's family taught her that she was never to quit a job that had good benefits, regardless of whether or not she liked the job. Quitting was simply not an option. She wanted more than anything to own a spa, so people could relax and be pampered. Her family's beliefs kept getting in the way. This stopped her from taking action and created much turmoil and unhappiness in her life. Simply waking up in the morning and thinking about going to her job as a manager in a clothing store that she hated made her feel sick to her stomach.

After months of working through this limiting belief, she quit her job and opened her spa. Once she left her job, she felt a heavy burden lift from her spirit. At first, her family let her know that they could not believe that she quit a good job that had great benefits. Ellen's response to them was, "I am sorry that you feel that way, but I have to do what is best for me." At that point, she was strong enough within herself to realize that other people's limiting beliefs no longer needed to stop her from pursuing what she wanted.

Ellen was very brave to continue to be true to herself, regardless of the criticism that she heard. Months after she opened her own business, she said that she could not believe how free and wonderful she felt. Not only does she love having her own spa, but she now looks forward to going to work every day! Ellen said that if she continued to believe that she could *not quit a job that had good benefits, she would have been miserable her whole life.*

> *"You have powers you never dreamed of.*
> *You can do things you never thought*
> *you could do. There are no*
> *limitations in what you can do except*
> *the limitations of your own mind."*
> — *Darwin P. Kingsley*

What action are you going to take over the next couple of weeks to get started with pursuing your heart's desires?

The steps that I am going to take over the next couple of weeks are:

1. _____
2. _____
3. _____
4. _____
5. _____

Make a commitment to follow through with taking these actions. If you do not take these actions over the next couple of weeks, then you are allowing your excuses to get in the way. Get rid of those excuses. Positive self-talk will do the trick. Tell yourself, "I need to support myself each day with working toward my heart's desires. I am no longer going to hold on to my excuses. It is time for me to create my heart's desires. I have everything that it takes to make these desires a reality." Keep doing positive self-talk each day. This will make a great difference in diminishing those excuses.

If it is in your heart to write a book, you may want to take action over the next couple of weeks by writing all your inspirational thoughts on paper. This is a good place to start. When you realize a few weeks later that you did not write one word on paper and you tell yourself that you have been too busy, that is an excuse. Perhaps fear and doubt are getting in the way. At that point tell yourself, "It is in my heart to write this book. I need to take action and keep writing. I have everything that it takes to make this happen. I am no longer going to let fear or doubt stand in my way."

You are now ready to create your heart's desires! Move forward each day as you make this happen. As you work toward these desires, know that you will be an inspiration to everyone around you. Wouldn't it be great if everyone you know also pursued their heart's desires because you modeled to them how to do so? If everyone pursued their heart's desires, this world would be a much better place.

We are all put on this earth for a reason. Have you ever witnessed how someone's life instantly changed because it was in another person's heart to help them? You may have personally experienced this yourself. I am deeply touched every time I witness this happening. Do you know that those people could have made excuses for not helping others? Thank goodness they did not. Throw away your excuses!

While you are in the tunnel, the only action you may need to take is being kind and loving toward yourself as you heal, and grow. Once you are out of that place, you will be rejuvenated, energized, and ready to pursue your heart's desires. If for some reason you have something solidly in your heart while you are in the tunnel, take action. I wish that I did that, so that I could have seen my old friend Joanne one more time before her life ended.

CHAPTER 14

How to Get Rid of Minor Annoyances

"Eternal inner peace has to be cultivated daily."
— *Delphine-Gay de Girardin*

Minor annoyances can quickly drain your energy, irritate you, lead to frustration, and create turmoil. Life is not meant to be lived this way. These irritations will linger until you get rid of them. As you work toward creating a happy life, you will need to block anything that drains your energy. Even as you heal, getting rid of minor annoyances will help you to feel empowered. What are some minor annoyances that you experience daily, weekly, monthly? How long have you had them? Sometimes we hold on to things that drain our energy in order to punish ourselves. I once had a leak in my workout room for over nine months! That leak bothered me every time I saw it. I kept making excuses for not calling a roofer. Finally, after I came back from a short trip that rejuvenated my spirit, I decided to get rid of everything that drained my energy. I called a roofer the next day and the problem was fixed in less than one hour! Plus, the roofer barely charged me anything to fix the problem.

Take action and put an end to as many annoyances as possible. Start small, get rid of the easier annoyance first and work your way toward getting rid of the bigger ones. You will feel less stress when you get in the habit of instantly zapping them. Once you do this, you will feel great! This is simply an act of self-love. The more you love who you are, the more fun, joy, and peace you will have in your life. When you do nothing to get rid of the things that continue to irritate you when you can, you are choosing to keep yourself in a bad state. At that point, ask yourself, "Why do I have a need to punish myself in this way?"

A few years ago, it seemed as though my minor annoyances kept multiplying by the week. A large portion of a tree fell in my yard after it got hit by lightning. My central air conditioner completely stopped working during a heat wave and the whole unit needed to be replaced. My cleaning ladies broke my window. I will not bore you, but I have to say that there were about fifteen other minor annoyances that occurred within a couple of months! Yes, I felt irritated by what was happening. Not many people would enjoy having carpenter ants walk freely through their house as though they were important guests. As the ants enjoyed the warmth of my home, they had many sips of water in the middle of my kitchen since the ceiling was leaking from a broken pipe.

After another tree fell in my yard around the same time when all the other minor annoyances developed, I just laughed. I eventually realized that I needed to develop a good attitude. From that point on, my new motto was, "Get rid of the minor annoyances as fast as possible." This motto has served me well. Do not let things drain your energy. You will feel empowered every time you get rid of the things that irritate you. The first week that I looked at the repaired ceiling in my kitchen and in my workout room, I felt great knowing that the leaks were fully gone.

If you are like most people, you have encountered minor annoyances while running errands. Perhaps you have had to stand on long lines, many times, at the post office or the grocery store. You may have felt uncomfortable feelings while you were there. You have options. You can get rid of those irritations as well. You may discover that if you run your errands at a different time or on a different day, you will avoid those long lines. Perhaps people are more pleasant at your favorite store at a different location. Treat yourself well by putting yourself in environments that feel good to you!

I find that there are some places by my office where workers tend to be much friendlier and more pleasant than where I live, so I do my errands at those places. This small change has made a big difference in my life. Not only do I actually enjoy food shopping, getting my car washed, going to the post office, and getting gas, but I also save time. I found a gas station that is open late, where the attendant, Moe, is so friendly and pleasant. It is always a pleasure to see him. He will always say to me with a big friendly smile on his face, "Norma, how have you been?" This is much better than having to wait on a long line where the attendants clearly show you that they would rather be anywhere but at work. My small decision of finding a gas station where I was comfortable getting gas has paid off. Little did I know before I made that decision that I could actually enjoy getting gas. I used to dread getting gas by my house because the attendants acted as though I were inconveniencing them by wanting gas. Once I decided to take great care of myself even in small ways, this freed me from unnecessary frustration and stress. Many of my patients have benefited from taking great care of themselves in these ways, too.

Some changes that will add to your life may be a little harder to make than others. Around the time Ali began a devastating divorce proceeding, when she found out her husband had been cheating on her, her hairdresser turned her hair black after she'd wanted it dyed dark blonde. The anger and sadness about her divorce made the annoyance of her hair looking "terrible" push her over the edge, and Ali decided "I can't make nice anymore." She knew she needed to take control of her life and no longer tolerate what wasn't working for her. The situation added temporary stress in Ali's life since the hairdresser and her family were old friends. However, Ali realized that she no longer needed to be dissatisfied with how her hair looked every time she left the salon. Twelve years was long enough. She switched to a new hairdresser, who always does a great job. Though her old hairdresser is no longer speaking to her, Ali's only regret is not waking up to this way of thinking sooner. It could have saved her from countless instances of being upset and annoyed in her life.

How about you: Are you unhappy with some type of service that you have been receiving? If so, it may be time to find someone new. Take small steps every day to get rid of minor annoyances. If you are unable to instantly rectify them, then why not ask your family and friends to help you get rid of them? Not only will you feel great about saying good-bye to those irritations, but others will feel great about helping you. In order to get rid of those irritations permanently, you need to first identify what they are.

How to Get Rid of Minor Annoyances

The five minor annoyances that I would like to get rid of are:

1. _____
2. _____
3. _____
4. _____
5. _____

I am going to get rid of these annoyances by:

_____
_____
_____
_____
_____

> *"People are born for different tasks, but in order to survive everyone requires the same nourishment: inner peace."*
> — *Sri Sathya Sai Baba*

Now that you have identified the things that drain your energy and how to get rid of them, you will need to take action. Remember, life rewards action! You have much bigger things to focus on than the negative impact that your minor annoyances offer. A healed person does not continue to swim in a pool of negativity. Instead, they swim in an ocean of possibilities and freedom. There is nothing freeing about holding on to things that drain you. Set yourself free and enjoy your renewed energy!

PART VI

Living a Life Filled with Joy

CHAPTER 15

How to Get Rid of "Joy Squashers"

When John came to me for counseling, he could not understand why he experienced so little joy in life. I could. His constant worry, anxiety, and depression stemming from unresolved childhood issues squashed his joy. John's father had been verbally and physically abusive to him throughout his childhood, often threatening to hurt John if he did not do what he asked. Until the day his father died, when John was twenty-one, he was afraid his father was "going to go after" him.

As I helped him work through his wounds, he began to experience joy. It was a strange new feeling at first, but now he is comfortable doing the things he loves. Today he is experiencing much joy by taking guitar lessons, playing volleyball, and surfing on the weekends.

If you are currently going through a difficult time, your feelings will temporarily get in the way of your being able to fully experience joy. But find the small moments of joy: a walk on a sunny day, hearing birds cheerfully sing, or seeing a beautiful sunset. When you are feeling better, make it a top priority to experience as many small moments of joy as you can. There are countless ways to do that, but first you need to get rid of your "joy squashers"—those things that stop you from feeling joyful.

First, take an honest look at how *you* might be squashing joy from your life. After all, we can't change what we don't acknowledge. Circle all the ways in the following list in which you have squashed your joy over the past year. There is no shame in acknowledging these feelings and actions, so don't hold back!

Joy Squashers

Living in fear
Worrying
Beat myself up with thoughts/words
Being overwhelmed
Being stressed
Letting my ego get in the way
Abusing myself
Accepting mistreatment
Mistreating others
Not saying no when I need to
Negative thinking

Negative actions
Not pursuing my heart's desires
Trying to be perfect
"Ignoring" my feelings
Having to be right
Blaming others
Focusing on what I do not have
Focusing on what is wrong
Not living in the moment
Being hard on myself
Comparing myself to others

I have also squashed my joy by:

_____

_____

_____

_____

_____

_____

If you circled and wrote down all the ways you can think of, it will be easy to see why there may be very little joy in your life. Are you surprised by how many ways you squash your own joy? You are not alone! Most of us do so in many ways each and every day.

Now that you've taken an honest look at what you have been doing, you can change that pattern with surprisingly simple yet very effective tools. Let's start by discussing each of the joy squashers in the list. A whole new world of possibilities is about to open up for you!

Living in Fear

Lindsay intuitively knew that her life was about to change for the better. Yet, she was terrified. Every time she thought about moving and changing her career, enormous fear would envelop her. She was scared of change. The only way she could diminish this fear was by praying, meditating, and doing positive self-talk.

Does this sound familiar? Are you living in fear? Do you experience fear daily? Do you know that 90 percent of your fears will never come to pass? That 90 percent is really about FALSE EVIDENCE APPEARING REAL. The only reason humans need to feel fear is when faced with an ACTUAL THREAT of danger. In such a case, you would need to follow your intuition and take good care of yourself.

Whenever you are in a fearful state without any threat of danger, you are not having faith. This negative emotion can have a debilitating effect on your body, mind, and spirit. It often rears its head when you are vulnerable, stressed, or overwhelmed, or when some need of yours is not being met. Your negative thoughts can throw open the floodgates, sending fear pouring through your mind and body. People learn in childhood to be afraid because their parents lived in fear. The good news is that what you learned in childhood can be unlearned in adulthood.

Feeling good, peaceful, and strong will help keep that negative emotion at bay. Thinking positively will also help. Your thoughts have the power to instantly diminish fear. Seem unlikely? The next time you experience that emotion, comfort yourself with your thoughts and words and see how quickly your fear dissipates.

River Meditation

An exercise that can quickly destroy baseless fear is what I call The River Meditation. Slowly take three deep breaths in and out. With each exhale, you are becoming more relaxed. You are now walking in the woods. There are tall, beautiful trees all around you. You feel a great sense of peace as you walk toward the river that is patiently waiting to destroy your fear. Once you come within a few feet of the water, see your fear pour out of your body in the form of various colors and into the river. Keep releasing this emotion until it is completely out of your body. Take a deep breath in and slowly exhale.

When that emotion is completely gone, see white light surround your body. You now feel great peace. Take in the light even more. Once you reach the state of total peace, keep yourself in this state for as long as you can, then slowly come back in the room. Before you open your eyes, know that this peace is yours. No one can take it away from you in this moment. If new fears begin to emerge, get rid of them, too, by repeating this meditation.

Fear Box

Another powerful way to get rid of fear is to give it away. Whenever you experience fear, write what is keeping you in this state on strips of paper and put them into a small box. Once they are in the box, know that they no longer belong to you; they belong to the box. Tell yourself, "This no longer belongs to me; it now belongs to the box. I have nothing to fear since fear is *false evidence appearing real.*" If you continue to experience this emotion, keep doing the exercise until it is fully gone.

Worrying

When Erica's sixteen-year-old son, Harrison, started driving, she became consumed with worry that he was going to get in an accident and die. Even though Harrison was a careful driver, her worries increased every time Harrison went behind the wheel. You know that worrying is useless and does absolutely no good, yet you continue to do it. Have you ever asked yourself, "Why am I worrying when this serves no purpose?" When you are struggling to trust, then you are likely to experience this emotion. In order to stop worrying, you will need to replace your negative thoughts with comforting ones. When you are going through some type of difficulty, remind yourself, "This difficult situation is only temporary. I am experiencing this difficulty because I am being prepared for something greater." The more you comfort and encourage yourself with your thoughts, the less this negative emotion will appear.

Another powerful way to end worrying is by feeding your spirit, which is in need of nourishment. This can bring you from a negative to a positive state in less than ten minutes. Try this experiment: the next time you worry, comfort yourself with your thoughts, then feed your spirit by reading something inspirational, listening to music that uplifts you, talking to a loved one, praying, meditating, relaxing, seeing yourself having everything you want, focusing on your blessings, or simply reminding yourself to trust. Once you take this action, say good-bye to that unwanted emotion. The results may not last too long at first, but the more you practice taking care of yourself, the longer the results will last.

Whenever life throws Ping-Pong balls at you, why not let your thoughts, actions, and words swat them away? The more you get in the habit of doing this, the faster you will get rid of them. You have the power within you to slowly destroy this emotion. Just focus on getting rid of one ball at a time. Do this by gathering your thoughts and writing them down.

What have you been worrying about over the past month?

_____

_____

_____

_____

What do you need to tell yourself in order to swat this emotion away?

_____

_____

_____

_____

How are you going to feed your spirit when you start to worry?

1._____   6._____

2._____   7._____

3._____   8._____

4._____   9._____

5._____   10._____

What actions do you need to take in order to decrease this negative emotion?

1._____

2._____

3._____

Now that you have some tools to help you, get in the good habit of doing these things often, and learn to trust. You may be facing a situation where it feels nearly impossible to stop experiencing this emotion. Perhaps a loved one is sick or someone you know is suffering. Worrying has negative power. Nothing good will ever come from it. You may think that by worrying, you will somehow be in control of a situation. You are not. All you are doing is hurting yourself. You may also think that by worrying, you are being helpful. You are not! You cannot be at peace and experience joy when you are in this lower state. Instead of spending your time that way, why not spend your time being positive? Positive thoughts, actions, and behaviors have the power to produce positive results.

Beating Myself Up with Thoughts or Words

Susie could not wait to go on her dream vacation: a cruise to Bermuda. As the cruise ship disembarked, she felt sheer joy. She was finally free from everything. Free from work, bills, running errands, cooking, cleaning, taking care of her elderly parents, running two households, and having to wait to be seen by another doctor. Her joy continued until the next morning when she realized that she could barely fit into her summer clothes that had been tucked away all winter. From that moment on, she was horrified that she had gained weight. She told herself that she looked terrible and that she was too embarrassed to be seen by anyone on the cruise. Susie continued to beat herself up with her thoughts every time she looked in the mirror or saw a picture or herself; therefore, her self-criticism tossed her joy overboard. Does this sound familiar? Have you had the chance to experience great joy, but instead you beat the joy out of you?

What you tell yourself will have a great impact on your life. If you tell yourself that you are a no-good piece of garbage, then you will certainly feel that way and instantly squash your joy. That is a lie! Start telling yourself the truth, "I am worthy of good." Once you believe this simple truth, your life will never be the same. Every time a negative thought about yourself or another person appears, see a Stop sign in your mind and replace your negative thoughts with positive ones.

Reprogramming your thinking will take work. But the more you work at it, the easier it will get. Keep focusing on thinking positively and speaking positively until this becomes a natural part of your life. It took me a while to reprogram my negative, defeatist thinking. Now, whenever I have a negative thought, I am able to zap it instantly and switch to a positive thought. Years ago, whenever I had one negative thought, that would open the floodgates to hours of negative thinking. Getting rid of negative thoughts saves me from so much turmoil. By now, you know that negative thoughts and words create not only fear and worry, but inner turmoil. You will discover that thinking positively and speaking positively will keep you in a good state of mind, which will naturally create inner peace.

Mirror Work

A powerful way to get rid of negative self-talk is by doing mirror work. Take this list and read each one of these in the mirror, one at a time. Pay attention to which messages are the most uncomfortable for you to say to yourself and believe. Then place a small check next to each message that you have trouble believing about yourself.

I am beautiful on the inside and outside.   I love my body.
I deserve to be happy.   I am loving and loveable.
I am a wonderful person.   I am kind.   I am worthy.   I am valuable.
I am smart.   I deserve to live a peaceful life.   I am talented.
I am capable.   I am successful.   I am good enough.
I am proud of myself.   I can accomplish my heart's desires.
I am intelligent.   I deserve all of life's good.
 I can do whatever I put my mind to.   I am competent.

Which messages were the most difficult for you to believe? Take three of those messages that you placed a check next to and say them every day. After you start to believe those messages, go back to your list and say the next three messages. Keep doing this until you believe everything that is written.

Give it a try! This technique is a powerful way to erase those old nasty tapes you have acquired throughout your life that keep playing in your head. Those negative tapes only block you from feeling good about yourself. If you do mirror work for a couple of months, while repeating your positive affirmations daily, you will start to believe your new messages. It may feel silly at first, but it works!

Being Overwhelmed

Gene felt overwhelmed often by all of his responsibilities and lack of joy. He tried not to feel this way, but he simply had too much on his plate. His new job and plans with family and friends consumed his every waking moment. Gene soon discovered that the only way he was not going to be overwhelmed was by making fewer plans until his big project at work was complete and by delegating some of his responsibilities. Immediately after Gene took the necessary action, he felt peaceful and experienced joy, which had not been a part of his life for nearly a year.

When you are overwhelmed, it means that at least one of your needs is not being met. Check in with yourself by asking these two simple questions, "Are all of my needs being met at this moment?" If the answer is no, then ask, "What need is currently not being met?" If you have been very busy, then you may have a need to rest. Make it a top priority to identify your needs and meet them. You will be shielding yourself to a large degree from being overwhelmed.

> *"Rest is not idleness, and to lie sometimes on the grass under trees on a summer's day, listening to the murmur of the water, or watching the clouds float across the sky, is by no means a waste of time."*
> *— J. Lubboc*

If you feel overwhelmed by the number of things that you need to do, why not prioritize what absolutely needs to get done? Ask yourself, "What must I do today?" and do only those things. It may be helpful to do one thing at a time and take a break after each task. If you need to do a few things in one day, do those things and then reward yourself. For instance, if you need to wash your car, go grocery shopping, and mow the lawn, reward yourself afterward by listening to your favorite music for a half hour. If you dread doing something, then give yourself an immediate reward after you accomplish the task. Tell yourself, "After I pay my bills, I am going to take a hot bath." Be sure to give yourself the reward even if the task ends up not being so dreadful. No matter what, if you are doing too much, you are going to be overwhelmed. You may need to slow down the pace of your life and not take on so much. Perhaps you need to practice saying no more often, so that you are not so overwhelmed.

Being Stressed

By devoting ten minutes a day to some de-stressing techniques, such as visualization or deep breathing, you no longer need to be weighed down by stress. If you can't even manage ten minutes on some days, then try this five-minute meditation.

Vacuum Meditation

Sit or lie in a comfortable place. Gently close your eyes and take in a deep breath. Notice the color of the stress that is surrounding your body. It may be red, black, gray, orange, or some other color. Above your head is a large vacuum hose. The hose is now powerfully absorbing your stress and any feelings that have been blocking you from being peaceful. After the vacuum absorbs everything that has been weighing you down, it is going to shoot up to the sky and explode into a beautiful white light. See white sparkles flutter down from the sky.

Take another deep breath in and relax even more. White light is now surrounding your body. Feel the joy that automatically comes from connecting to this light. Now the light is expanding even more. Take in as much joy as you can. When you are ready, slowly come back in the room. Feel your feet on the floor. Hear any sounds that are in the room. Gently open your eyes. Notice how much better you feel!

Letting My Ego Get in the Way

Scott told his girlfriend, Carmen, that she was the love of his life. He confessed his love for her to his family, friends, and co-workers.

After five months of dating, during an argument, Scott told Carmen that he knew he had an ego and that he was not going to change. His ego cost him his relationship. Whenever Carmen reminded Scott that she did not appreciate him cursing and yelling at her for something as simple as accidentally spilling coffee, he would say, "too bad, I am not going to change." Scott always had to have the last word and make a big deal out of the smallest things that went wrong. Even though Carmen cared for Scott, she knew after six months of dating him that he truly was not going to change; therefore, she ended the relationship. She was no longer willing to tolerate the unnecessary turmoil that his ego continued to create in their relationship.

Our egos often appear the strongest when we are hurting on the inside. You may not even be aware of the feelings that you have not been able to experience for years. Your ego has kept them hidden. Only a very courageous person will acknowledge and feel their feelings. You are that courageous person! You are not meant to wear a mask. This will not do a bit of good for you or for anyone. This mask will become a repellent in all of your relationships. No one feels uplifted being around someone who is a phony or thinks he or she is better than others. Whenever you control or put someone down, gossip, think that you are better than anyone, or lie in order to look good, your ego is in action.

It will also be in action when you tell yourself that you do not need to grow or change in any way. You cannot be at peace when you are operating from such a place. Whenever you use that ugly mask, you are in a fearful state. Great things cannot come from living in fear! If you are defensive when someone is kindly giving you constructive feedback, it's your ego again. When you are no longer operating this way, you will be able to grow fully and your life will be much more peaceful.

Abusing Myself

Jennie was an attractive, smart, and well-liked senior in high school. On the outside, it seemed as though her life was perfect. What people did not know was that she was unable to see anything good about herself. Her self-hatred was obvious only to her. She would often abuse herself through bingeing/purging, and convincing herself that she was worthless. Instead of spending time with her friends after school and on weekends, Jennie spent her time driving to the nearest store and purchasing whatever food she wanted to eat, only later to make herself purge.

She knew that her self-hatred was destroying her life. Once Jennie learned in counseling to like herself and worked through many feelings, a new life began to emerge. Her abusive behavior toward herself ended and her relationships blossomed, as well as her joy.

If you don't like yourself, then the chances are that you are doing something often, if not every day, that is abusive toward yourself. Do you have any addictions? Does that critical voice in your head constantly put you down or call you wrong? Do you continue to make choices that make you feel terrible? You cannot live a peaceful, joyous life if you abuse yourself in any way.

Accepting Mistreatment

I find that many individuals struggle with this issue, often blaming themselves when someone mistreats them. No one has the right to mistreat you! There are many wonderful people in this world who will treat you with love, kindness, and respect if you give them a chance. However, you need to make room for these people to enter your life. I have certainly had this experience. For years, I allowed people to mistreat me because I did not feel good enough about myself. Once I put an end to all mistreatment, I was amazed to see that fantastic people just walked into my life. The same will happen to you if you allow it.

When someone is hurting you, whether through verbal, emotional, sexual, or physical abuse, you must assert yourself and put an end to that abuse. Sometimes this means permanently ending a relationship, if the abuse does not stop. You know that any form of abuse feels horrible. Do not talk yourself out of going for help if you are being abused. Get the help you need. Remember, you do not deserve to be mistreated by *anyone*.

Mistreating Others

Bob was well respected at work. People thought he was "such a nice guy." His mother did not think so, especially since he continued to yell and curse at her for "irritating" him. Even though Bob's wife would often gently tell him that he had no right to treat his mother that way, he ignored her.

Just as there are numerous ways in which you can mistreat yourself, there are numerous ways in which you can mistreat others. If you are abusive verbally, emotionally, physically, or sexually, then seek professional help. You will not be able to be peaceful and live a good life if you are hurting yourself or anyone else. You may have made poor choices in the past, but that doesn't mean you need to continue those choices in your life today. You have the power within you to start a whole new journey at this very moment. If you have been abusing others, know that you are not alone. There are millions of people who have also done this. But you have the responsibility at this very second to stop being abusive and seek help.

Not Saying No When I Need To

Gabrielle asked her new friend, Hope, if she wanted to meet her in the city for lunch on Friday. Hope knew that that would not work for her since she had too many things to do that day. Instead of saying no to her new friend, she said "Sure, I would love to meet you in the city for lunch." As Hope was on her way to meet Gabrielle at the restaurant, she parked her car in a parking garage and then realized that it was a private lot. She had no way of getting out since the entrance gate was locked and no one was in the booth to help her. She then panicked and scratched the whole side of her car trying to find a way out. Not saying no to Gabrielle when she needed to created an enormous amount of stress. This lesson reminded Hope that her people-pleasing days needed to be over.

Has being a people-pleaser gotten in the way of being able to say no to the things that are not right for you? Perhaps you are afraid that you will disappoint someone or hurt their feelings if you are assertive in this way.

Even worse, you continue to deny yourself because you are afraid that you may be abandoned if you stop pleasing everyone. You have the right to assert yourself when something is not right for you! It can be helpful to practice saying no to smaller things before you tackle the bigger ones.

If someone asks you to answer some questions for a survey that you do not want to do, you can say "No, thanks, but have a good day." If the sales clerk asks if you want to save 10 percent by opening another credit card you do not want, say, "No, thank you." By simply being assertive, you will be free from all the turmoil and stress that arise when you go against your inner truth.

A healed person can say no easily, even if this means not pleasing others. It is not healthy to put your needs aside so that you can be a people-pleaser. It is wonderful to be giving, but not when it's at your expense and you are left feeling depleted and drained. Do you find that you are trying to please others in order to win their approval? Once you approve of yourself, you will no longer desperately seek the approval of others.

At first, you will be very uncomfortable saying no to things you used to do but didn't want to. That's okay. Allow yourself to temporarily feel this way. I have witnessed many people who were very uncomfortable being assertive at first but now are able to say no as though they have been doing it their entire life. Whenever anyone asks you a question, listen to what your inner voice has to say before you give an answer. This will help you to be assertive. If you are unable to quickly get in touch with that part of yourself, then buy yourself some time. You can say, "Let me think about that and I will get back to you." Then focus on seeing what feels right to you. The more you are in tune with your inner voice, the easier it will be to listen to what it has to say.

Keep in mind that when you first start saying no, people may feel threatened by your new assertiveness. They are simply not used to you acting this way. Do not let anyone's reaction take away from listening to your intuition and taking good care of yourself, however. In time, people will get used to your being "in your power."

Negative Thinking and Negative Actions

All Bethenny longed for in life was to find a wonderful husband. However, Bethenny told herself that she was not "good enough" or "pretty enough" to join a matchmaking service. Whenever a nice gentleman would ask her out, she would decline the offer and immediately find fault with him. Her negative thinking about herself continued to stop her from taking the action she needed to take in order to have what she wanted.

The fastest way to destroy all forms of joy is by thinking negatively. It's like taking a bat and beating that positive emotion out of you. You just found out that you are getting an unexpected check in the mail. You are excited! This gives you joy. You think of how you are going to spend that money. After all, it is free money. Then you have a negative thought that you should have received an even bigger check. In that moment, you instantly squashed your joy.

Negative thinking will also create negative actions and outcomes. This vicious cycle often occurs because you developed this ugly habit many years ago. It takes only twenty-one days to form a new habit. By beginning today to think positively, you have only twenty more days to go before you develop one of the most beneficial habits you will ever have!

When was the last time you felt great joy? What did you tell yourself that helped you to do that? People who savor their joy feel worthy and good about themselves. If you continue not to like yourself, then you will continue to squash your own joy. You will simply take out your emotional bat and use it on yourself over and over. When you get rid of your negative thinking, you will also get rid of that bat that you have been carrying around for years. Aren't you tired of beating good feelings out of yourself? Once you get rid of this destructive behavior, you are going to feel much better and it will become easier for you to keep your thoughts and actions positive; therefore, you will experience more joy!

Not Pursuing My Heart's Desires

When Ashley was sixteen, she dropped out of high school after she became pregnant. For forty-eight years, it was in her heart to earn her GED. After Ashley's new friend encouraged her to pursue her heart's desire, she did. Every time Ashley thinks about having her GED, she feels great joy. Ashley wishes that she pursued her heart's desire many years ago.

One of the most powerful ways to experience joy is by pursuing and obtaining your heart's desires. Without them, you are likely to feel that something is missing in your life; your passion and joy will be missing.

Support yourself with bringing your heart's desires to fruition. Remind yourself that you are well equipped to make your heart's desires a reality. Now the choice is yours. You can either work toward making them a reality or continue to float through life with no direction. Ignoring your dreams will leave you feeling empty. Pursue what is meant for your life and get ready for more joy!

Trying to Be Perfect

"The thing that is really hard and really amazing is giving up on being perfect and beginning the work of becoming yourself."
— Anna Quindlen

Wendy could not stand to be in her own skin whenever she was not perfect. Terror often filled her heart whenever she made a mistake. Her perfection issue was so severe that even when everything was good in her life, she felt complete turmoil from not being perfect. Do you put pressure on yourself to be perfect? You will never be perfect, no matter how hard you try, because you are human. You are good enough as you are! Stop putting the unrealistic expectation of perfection on yourself. Whenever you do this, YOU ARE NOT LOVING YOURSELF! I have counseled numerous individuals who have suffered from trying to be perfect. I have also struggled with this issue for many years, so I know how painful and debilitating it can be. Great freedom comes when you stop this behavior.

The way to begin to change this behavior is by loving yourself. When you love and accept yourself, you will no longer try to be something that you are not.

"Ignoring" My Feelings

Robin had been molested by her grandfather when she was a little girl. Throughout her teen years and early adulthood, she continued to ignore her feelings and stuff them by eating excessively. Her obesity made her feel even worse about herself and life. Robin decided to feel her feelings, rather than medicate them with food. As she worked through her feelings, her weight started to come off. When you have been through a lot, you will have many feelings that need to be felt before you can fully heal. You may try to wish them away, or "stuff" them. Unfortunately, that never works. Your difficult feelings will diminish only when you experience them. Once you process all those stuffed feelings, joy will occupy the empty space within.

Having to Be Right

Ryan created much turmoil in his relationships because he always had to be right. When his teenage daughter was talking on the phone in her room, he insisted that she was hiding something from him. The truth was that she wanted some privacy. No matter how many times Cynthia explained that she just wanted privacy, her father insisted that she was hiding something and punished her for a week.

Ryan was missing out on the possibility of having a good relationship with the most important people in his life. His need to make everyone wrong was more important to him than anything; he would rather be right than be happy and have fulfilling relationships. When Cynthia yelled at her father out of anger that she and everyone hated that he always had to be right, Ryan became emotional. In that moment, he realized that he was treating others the way that his abusive mother had treated him. It took much healing before Ryan could give up his need to be right. Once he did, his relationships became more peaceful and satisfying.

We live in a world where most people will do anything to prove that they are right, regardless of the damage it may cause. Being a well-informed person is great, but if you *have to* be right, you will suffocate your relationships and never achieve a life of joy. A healthy person feels good enough about him- or herself to admit a mistake, apologize, and work on not making the same mistake again.

A wounded person will hold on to being right in order to feel some sense of control in their life. Without this sense of control, they would be forced to feel their feelings and let go of their ego. That's too scary, so they justify their need to prove everyone wrong. When you have to prove everyone wrong, you are holding on to false power. This is the ego's way of saying, "I am good and you are bad. I am right and you are wrong. I am superior and you are inferior." No one enjoys being around anyone who operates this way. Guess what? You do not have to be right all the time. In fact, you will never be. This does not make you a bad person. Real growth occurs when you give up having to be right. Once you give up this false way of being by reminding yourself over and over that *you do not always have to be right* and allow yourself to admit your mistakes, you will be open to experiencing peace and joy.

Blaming Others

Holly would often tell me that her mother should pay for her counseling since she made her life miserable. Holly was stuck in blame. Her mother had been abusive toward her when she was a little girl; however, she needed to move beyond blame so that she could heal and forgive, which would allow her to be emotionally free from the past. Most people want to blame someone else when things don't turn out right. Are you doing this because someone hurt you? Perhaps you do not want to give up the blame because that will mean that what someone did to hurt you is all right. There is nothing all right about anyone hurting you, but being stuck in this negative emotion will only keep you stuck in life and stop you from experiencing joy.

If your parents shoved food down your throat for years and you had two hundred extra pounds of weight as a result of that abuse, you would then need to take control of your life and lose that weight. You can continue walking around blaming your parents for what they did. That will get you nowhere. You can also choose to heal through your suffering and forgive them. Then your weight will drop and you will be free.

The same is true with any type of awful experience you have been through. Slowly heal from the impact this experience had on your life, forgive, and you will be free. You may be too angry at this point to stop blaming someone for your circumstances. If you have the need to blame others, then do so for only a short period of time. When you are ready to release this emotion and forgive, you will set yourself free to experience the joy that is patiently waiting for you!

Focusing On What I Do Not Have

You can have an amazing life and still be very unhappy if you focus on what you do *not* have. This is yet another way to squash your joy and disregard your blessings. *Liz had an adoring husband, a wonderful family, a great career, and a beautiful home, but that was not enough for her. She was obsessed with having a baby. Most of her thoughts and actions revolved around trying to get pregnant. For three years, she made everyone's life miserable by telling them how her life was so terrible since she did not have a baby. Her negativity was toxic. By focusing on what she did not have, Liz made no room for joy.*

Why not focus on how blessed you are, so that you can feel good? If there is something in your heart that you don't have, then work toward taking the necessary steps to make it a reality. As you take those steps, focus your attention on all the things you do have, while making what you don't have smaller in your mind. By changing your perspective in this way, you will be giving yourself the gift of peace and joy.

Focusing On What Is Wrong

When you focus on what is right in your life, you will experience great joy. You can have everything in the world and be miserable if you focus on the one thing that is wrong. There are people who have very little, and yet they are living a life of joy. That is because they focus on the good in their lives. They turn up this volume in their minds, while keeping the volume of their struggles turned low.

Irene is a good example. She is a single mother of two who barely has enough money, time, or energy to meet some of her basic needs. Instead of focusing on how overwhelming and exhausting it is for her to raise two children completely on her own, Irene focuses on how blessed she is to have them. She also focuses on small moments of joy as often as she can.

If you are unable to change what you do not like about your life, then you need to accept it and try to make it small in your mind. See what you do not like as the size of a pea, and see what is good in your life as large as a movie screen. Play what is right in your life on your movie screen. Hold on to this image throughout your day. Once you master focusing on what is right while making what is wrong very small in your mind, you will automatically feel more joy.

Not Living in the Moment

After Karen's divorce, her anxiety and stress about being on her own for the first time in her life terrified her. Her terror stopped her from living in the moment. Karen's mind was too consumed with what was going to happen in the future. By not living in the moment, she was unable to experience the joy that her blessings had to offer. As Karen and I worked to decrease her stress and anxiety, she was able to live in the moment and experience more joy than she had ever experienced in her life. Instead of focusing on the future, she focused on her children, grandchildren, her friends, and doing all the things that brought her joy. Today, she is living a life of peace, joy, and happiness.

It is wise to plan for your future; however, when you live in the future you cannot be fully present to your life today. The same is true with living in the past. When most of your thoughts revolve around the past, then you cannot be fully present to your life today. In reality, YOU HAVE NO FUTURE or PAST in this present moment; all you have is NOW! If you live in the NOW, then you will be free to enjoy each day as much as possible. Make the most of your life now. Remember, all you have in life is this very second. If you have trouble living in the moment, then constantly remind yourself to focus on NOW. This will save you from much stress and turmoil. When you are healing, if you tell yourself to take one day at a time, one minute at a time, and even one second at a time, this will help you.

Being Hard on Myself

Angel is one of the most loving, kind, and generous people you could ever meet. Friends and strangers will often tell her that she is the nicest person they have ever met. What people do not know is that Angel is extremely hard on herself. If Angel does or says something that she judges as not being perfect or being wrong, she will beat herself up for days with her thoughts and, as a result, experience great emotional turmoil. Do you constantly make yourself wrong? As a young child, you may have heard someone say to you, "What did you do to make your sister cry?" Here it was assumed that you did something wrong, regardless of whether or not you had. Your teacher may have told you that you needed to stop talking to your classmate after you politely told your classmate that you would talk to her after class. You were once again made wrong. Most people have had such experiences. It is no wonder that we grow up into adults who automatically blame ourselves when something goes wrong.

Changing this pattern begins with the recognition that it exists. Focus on how you feel and what you tell yourself when something goes wrong. Do you automatically feel responsible and blame yourself? If you clearly did nothing wrong, then remind yourself of this truth: "I refuse to blame myself for this situation when I did not do anything wrong. I am no longer going to be hard on myself when I am innocent." You may need to repeat the truth over and over in your mind before you change your old pattern of blaming yourself. If you did do something wrong, then learn from that experience. Make sure you do not do that again, forgive yourself, and move forward.

Comparing Myself to Others

When I first started counseling Adrianne, a high school student, she felt very depressed because she was in the habit of comparing herself to her sister and to her peers. Adrianne's youngest sister excelled at everything and she was very popular. As Adrianne compared herself, she felt worthless and not good enough. Once she stopped this negative behavior, she started to see her good qualities. Adrianne realized that she was a good friend, student, and athlete.

As she started to see herself in a more positive light, she began to feel good about herself. As a result of her increased self-esteem, she made new friends, did better than ever in high school, and received a scholarship that she never would have dreamed a few years earlier of getting. Plus, she received several athletic awards. If Adrianne continued to compare herself to her sister and peers, she would never have had the confidence she needed to make new friends, apply for scholarships, and believe in her athletic abilities.

One of the quickest ways not to feel good and to squash your joy is by comparing yourself to others. There has never been anyone exactly like you and there never will be. Focus on your unique talents and abilities that are perfect only for YOU without telling yourself that you are not as good as someone else. Whenever you compare yourself to others, you are back to being emotionally abusive toward yourself and blocking your ability to see your good qualities. It is fantastic to admire something about someone, but do so without playing the comparison game.

So what if someone has a great shape and you are overweight? If you want to look your best, then make a commitment today to work toward that goal. If someone has a grand house unlike anything you are likely to ever afford, then make peace with what you have. This is your life exactly the way it was meant to be.

When you stop comparing yourself to others, then you will be able to see value in your unique self! A healthy person will not dare play the comparison game. Whenever this game is played, there is only one loser: you!

Life is not meant to be one big struggle after another. It is meant to be lived with peace and joy. Get rid of your joy squashers, so that you can experience the unlimited joy that is in store for you! You cannot live a joyous life if you continue to squash your joy. Once you get rid of your joy squashers, your whole new journey toward creating unlimited amounts of joy will begin. Being on this journey will be well worth all your efforts to get there. Let joy become a natural part of your life. You deserve it!

It Is Time to Live a Life of Joy

Sally intentionally focuses on living a life of joy, regardless of what obstacles come her way. She makes it a top priority each day to do at least one thing that brings her joy, whether it is reading something inspirational, spending time with someone she loves, or simply writing in her journal. As a result of experiencing much joy, she is positive and has a great attitude. Sally is one of the very few people at her job who loves her work. Whenever Sally hears one of her co-workers complain about the job, Sally will tell them that she does not want to hear anything negative about work. She will then tell them that she loves her job and is grateful to have it in the first place.

"Not what we have but what we enjoy constitutes our abundance."

*— **Epicurus***

Living a life of joy is more important than you realize. When you experience joy on a daily basis, this will help you to keep your attitude positive, along with your thoughts, feelings, and actions. Therefore, your state will be good and you will be resilient when facing life's challenges. Your resiliency will help you not to be discouraged, but to move forward with confidence and to support your belief in yourself. When you have faith and believe in yourself, then anything will be possible. People will be drawn to you since your inner light will be glowing. Nothing but good comes when you create more joy for yourself! When you feel good, not only will you be taking good care of yourself, but you will attract more good to you.

Now that you have identified and are ready to get rid of the joy squashers, it is time to add more joy to your life. To begin the next step, ask yourself this simple question, "What brings me joy?"

I experience joy when:

_____

_____

_____

_____

Perhaps you have never asked yourself that question. The truth is, deep down inside of you lies the answer. If you ponder this question long enough, an answer is likely to surface. Another way to identify what brings you joy is by asking yourself, "What am I passionate about?" Whenever there is passion, there is joy.

What have you been passionate about throughout your life? Are you passionate about helping people? How about nature? Do you have a passion for reading? Are you passionate about getting physically fit? Is traveling one of your passions?

I am passionate about:

_____

_____

_____

"Live your heart's passion.
Do whatever it is that excites your
inner light and passion. Live exuberantly
with purpose and excitement. Truly make your
life an adventure."
— Henry Leo Bolduc

If you are not sure what truly brings you joy, then it is time to try new things. Keep an open mind while making this discovery. If something makes you feel good, uplifts your spirit, or is fun for you, then it brings you joy. Take note of everything that you discover and keep adding to your list.

You may discover that what brought you joy as a child may also do so in your adult life. On my fifth birthday, my wonderful elderly neighbor, Helen, gave me an unexpected birthday gift. As I unwrapped the present, I discovered that it was a black jewelry box filled with big, gaudy jewelry that I absolutely loved. I was elated! How did she know that my favorite thing in the whole world, besides my little kittens, was jewelry? I could not believe my eyes. I had never at that point felt so much joy and excitement from receiving something! When I think back to that day, I can still feel the joy and elation that I felt the moment I unwrapped my present.

Think back to when you were a child. What brought you joy?

When I was a child, I felt joy when:

_____

_____

_____

_____

Creating an abundance of joy will require you to be open to all possibilities. I enjoy working out. I also enjoy socializing. For me, going to my gym brings me joy. Every time I am at the gym, I will see one of my acquaintances I really enjoy talking with. Some of my acquaintances have a natural ability to make people laugh. A few of them make everyone laugh! I know that I am fortunate to work out at a gym where most of the regulars genuinely like one another. Years ago, I never would have believed that I could experience so much joy at a gym.

Are you able to instantly add joy to your life on any given day? If I ever need to add instant joy to my day, all I have to do is go to Dunkin' Donuts and grab a cup of coffee. I have been visiting the same Dunkin' Donuts for years, so I get great joy out of saying "hi" to everyone and getting one of my favorite things, coffee. You are the only one who has the power to add instant joy to your life. Give this gift to yourself!

In addition to getting rid of your joy squashers, it is important not to allow anyone to squash your joy. Think of a time when you were feeling great joy and someone came along and popped your joy balloon. This can be very disappointing. You may have experienced that several times. I know I have. Years ago, I thought that everyone would be able to celebrate my joy. I quickly discovered that this was not true. I had the unfortunate experience in my early twenties of letting several people pop my balloons that I had worked hard to create. At that time, I knew that I was able to support people with their joy, so I assumed that others would support me with mine. I was wrong!

I no longer let anyone pop my balloon. I now safeguard it by only sharing with people who will support me. It is important to know which people in your life can do this. Safeguard your balloon! It belongs to you. If you are not sure who will support you, start off by sharing small joys with people and see how they respond. If no one in your life is able to support you, then make new friends who will. There are plenty of people who are capable of this. Get clear about the type of people you want in your life. Now come up with a plan where you can meet them. Your new friends are waiting for you! They will be glad to celebrate all your joys with you!

As I started to experience greater joy and happiness in my life, I wanted more friends who also lived their lives with great joy and happiness. Within one year, I was able to cultivate four new meaningful relationships! My new friends are just as motivated as I am to live an extraordinary life, not to mention that they are very supportive of my joy and happiness.

You are meant to live a wonderful life! Take baby steps as you work toward getting rid of the joy squashers. There is an unlimited amount of joy waiting for you! Allow yourself to experience this possibility more and more each day! Over time, your life will begin to flourish in ways you never dreamed possible.

PART VII

Living a Good Life

CHAPTER 16

Develop an Attitude of Gratitude

"Gratitude unlocks the fullness of life. It turns what we have into enough, and more. It turns denial into acceptance, chaos to order, confusion to clarity. It can turn a meal into a feast, a house into a home, a stranger into a friend. Gratitude makes sense of our past, brings peace for today, and creates a vision for tomorrow."

— *Melody Beattie*

How often do you focus on being grateful? If your answer is every day, then good for you! You are taking another necessary step toward creating an extraordinary life. All your talents, abilities, and positive attributes are something to be grateful for. If you have food on the table and somewhere to live, then you are blessed. Your hardship may consume you to the point where you are unable to see beyond your temporary suffering.

Some of the happiest people are the ones who focus on being grateful, regardless of what they actually have or what they have been through. When you shift your focus in this way, you will also be changing your mental state, where you feel more positive about life. When you are in a good state of mind, life seems to flow easily, without unnecessary struggle; therefore, you can allow peace to reside within you. Why not put yourself in a better state of mind each day by being grateful? Lots of good will be sent your way; you just need to accept it and say, "Thank you." The more you show sincere appreciation, the more you shall receive. Good things will come in different forms. You do not need to judge how they appear in your life. Whenever you do this, you stand the chance of either blocking it from entering your life or you may let it go and live a life full of regrets.

How do you view all the good in your life? Do you think negatively by saying to yourself, "I do not have that much good in my life because I certainly do not have what I want," or are you able to see the good in your life? Do you lose sight of the good things in your life because you focus on how others are more fortunate than you? This is a fast way to be miserable. If you ever want to see how much good you truly have in your life, going to a third world country will do the trick. When I was in India, I witnessed a mother bathe and brush her son's teeth in sewer water. At that moment, I realized just how blessed I am. For some people in India or any third world country, having a sheet hang over their heads, which they call home, is a good thing.

During my visit to a Christian hospital in India, where people were treated for free, I could not believe that hundreds of sick people had to wait for days and possibly weeks before they could see one of the two doctors on staff. Walking through the hospital and seeing all the suffering was one of the most disturbing experiences of my life. People were crying, moaning, and begging for someone to help them. I almost passed out a couple of times as I walked through the hospital because I could barely handle seeing and hearing everyone's suffering. It was heart-wrenching to witness the reality of these people's lives. A nurse told me that everyone at the hospital was fortunate since they were able to get to the hospital in the first place. There are many people in India who have no way of getting to the hospital at all. They have to endure their suffering without any help. The thought of this is completely disturbing. Whenever you read about or see on television how people in third world countries live, you know that you are blessed. However, when you are visiting a third world country, you cannot help but be utterly amazed to realize how much good is truly in your life.

My grandmother struggled for many years after her husband walked out on her and her eight children. She told me that even though she did not have any money, she had had faith that she would be fine. Before Grandma passed away, she said that if it were not for her faith, she never would have made it. Grandma mentioned that she only had one friend in her life, for a short period of time, and that she wished that she had more friends. This was very sad for me to hear and quite surprising. Grandma said that she never had any time to make friends because of having to raise her children and, years later, helped to raise some of her grandchildren. Grandma was an amazing person. She had very little in life and yet she was able to appreciate and be grateful for what she had.

I have counseled several patients who talked about how they were related to people who had everything anyone could possibly want in life and they were ungrateful, negative, and very unhappy. They chose to be miserable by not being grateful for what they had. Instead, they would continue to focus on everything that was wrong in their lives. My grandmother barely had a cent to her name and she was one of the most grateful people I have ever known. It was always a pleasure to be around Grandma since she was so loving and positive.

Are you able to see a doctor whenever you are sick? Do you have friends? Do you have a car? Are you able to see, touch, hear, smell? Then you have much to be grateful for. Even if you have health issues, you are blessed to be alive. You probably have an unbelievable amount of good in your life, but you forget to stay focused on that. Perhaps you feel sorry for yourself for not having what you want. The more you are grateful for the small things in life, seeing a beautiful sunset, playing the guitar—the more you will awaken to all the larger good things in your life, and those that are in store for you!

Take a few minutes to think about what you are grateful for.

I am grateful for:

_____
_____
_____
_____
_____
_____

"Gratitude is riches. Complaint is poverty."

— Doris Day

Even if you had a horrific childhood, there are some things you can be grateful for. The fact that you survived your childhood is one of those things. Did anyone show you love during your childhood? Now you have another thing to add to your list. *Mariah was blessed with two good friends during her horrific childhood filled with physical and sexual abuse. Mariah said, "I am grateful for their friendship." Even though she would leave school to return home to abuse from her father, Mariah was grateful that she had two friends who were always there for her the next morning.*

Teachers are another thing to be grateful for. *Jessica said that she was blessed during her childhood with some wonderful teachers who had big hearts. Her fifth-grade teacher, Mr. S, was one of those teachers. Jessica knew that she was one of his favorite students. What Mr. S did not know is that most of the time her mind was wandering somewhere else, because she had a hard time concentrating due to experiencing severe abuse at home. When Mr. S asked her if she wanted to be a crossing guard, she froze. She had no clue what he was asking. All she heard was him saying her name. Her friend whispered, "Say yes." She had no idea what she was saying yes to but she trusted that her friend would not steer her wrong. Later, Jessica discovered that she was asked to be a crossing guard, which was a big honor for her. A couple of weeks later, he also asked her if she wanted the privilege of decorating one of the bulletin boards in the hallway. This made her feel special.*

Right before Christmas break Jessica told Mr. S in the hallway that she loved him. To this day, she is glad that she told him this because when she was in sixth grade, he died of a heart attack. Jessica was completely crushed when she learned that her favorite person in the world had died. However, he will forever be in her heart.

What are you grateful for from your childhood?

_____

_____

_____

_____

_____

When Jill was nineteen, she attended a healing seminar for the weekend. Throughout the weekend, the facilitators helped all the attendees get in touch with deep, unhealed feelings. As Jill experienced deep pain regarding her grandparents passing away a few years earlier, one of the facilitators put her arms around her. At that moment, Jill's heart's desire was to have a grandmother like the elderly woman who hugged her. Jill felt great sadness; it was in her heart to have a loving grandmother but there was no way that she could ever have a grandmother at the age of nineteen. Even though Jill knew that she was never going to have her heart's desire, she secretly wished that she would.

One year after the seminar, a friend asked her if she wanted to make a little extra money cleaning for an elderly woman. Jill knew that for some reason she was supposed to take the position, but she did not know why, since she hated cleaning. She trusted her intuition and accepted the offer. Every time Jill finished cleaning for Betty, they would talk for long periods of time. Betty enjoyed hearing how Jill was doing in college. Over time, Jill and Betty formed a loving relationship. After a year, Jill was unable to clean for Betty any longer due to the demands of student teaching, classwork, and working on the weekends. Jill and Betty's bond was too strong at that time for them to simply say good-bye.

Over the years, Betty and Jill continued to spend much time together. Jill somehow became a part of Betty's family. Eventually, Betty became "Gram" and her husband, Sam, was "Grandpa." Jill was invited to many family functions. Betty's son, sister, nieces, and nephews opened their hearts to her. Everyone in Betty's family was loving and accepting of her. Jill said that she is so grateful for having had Betty in her life for thirteen years.

Throughout the years, Betty told Jill that she felt as though she had been her biological grandchild. Jill felt the same way. Betty meant the world to Jill. Even though Betty passed away, Jill still feels Betty's love and comfort. One year after Betty passed away, her son gave Jill four paintings that Betty had made. It was very difficult for Jill to fully face her loss, so she waited a solid year before she unwrapped her treasured gift.

Jill meditated before she began unwrapping. During her meditation, she imagined talking to Betty and asking her to describe one of the paintings that she had left her. Jill intuitively got that one of the paintings had several small boats, along with one very large boat, floating on the ocean. After she meditated, Jill laughed at herself. She knew that there was no way that she could talk to Betty.

After she laughed, Jill was ready to unwrap the brown paper that had securely protected the paintings. When she discovered what was under the paper, she could not believe her eyes. Jill saw small boats, along with one big boat floating on the ocean! In that moment, Jill realized that the love she and Betty had for each other was never going to die. Jill could have stopped herself from being open to having her heart's desire of having a loving grandmother. However, she kept an open mind to this possibility. Jill's experience taught her that even the seemingly impossible heart's desires can be fulfilled! She will be forever grateful for having that experience.

Take a few minutes to think about some of the experiences that you have had throughout your life that you are grateful for.

Some experiences I have had in my life that I am grateful for are:

_____

_____

_____

_____

_____

_____

_____

Give Thanks for the Good in Your Life

How often do you give thanks for the good in your life? When was the last time you quietly said thank you in your mind? If you go throughout life without gratitude, then how can you possibly see all the good that is in your life? You cannot. For me, experiencing the good in my life can be as simple as having a pleasant conversation with a neighbor, taking a walk in nature, or riding my bike. I am so grateful for all these things. Do you have a pet? Well, that is surely something to be grateful for! Once you get in the habit of saying "thank you" your view on life will change. You will truly begin to see, perhaps for the first time, how much good is in your life. If you are emotionally suffering, push yourself to focus on being grateful for anything that is good in your life so that you can fill your heart up with positive feelings. Sometimes this is the only thing that can help you to move forward with comfort. Allow this emotional medicine to comfort you when life feels dark and difficult.

The important thing to know is that you are meant to live a happy life. You just need to feel good enough about yourself to be open to receiving more good that is in store for you. If you do not feel good about yourself, you will likely fail to take the necessary steps to bring more good in your life. You may think, "I am not capable enough or smart enough to take that position, so I am not even going to apply for that job." Wham, you just threw a major opportunity in the gutter.

Even if something good is automatically positioned in your life, without you having to do a thing, you can easily talk yourself out of receiving it. "No, I am not going on a date with Emma's son; he seems too good to be true. He is well liked by everyone. He has a great job and he is very smart. I am sure that if I got to know him well enough, he would be just like all the other jerks I dated." How sad that this type of thinking can stop you from receiving what was intended for your life.

There will be times when you sense that something wonderful is coming your way, yet you do everything to sabotage this. How many times have you felt led to do something, but you ignored your inner voice? Perhaps you had an offer that you told yourself was too good to be true. "I am not going to write for that magazine. I will not bother asking how much I would get paid to write for them on a weekly basis. Forget it; I am not taking that offer. They probably want to take advantage of me because they heard my former boss say that I was one of the best writers on staff." Does this sound like you? Do you continue to talk yourself out of receiving something that you could be grateful for because it sounds too good to be true?

Life is about savoring and enjoying the good. Do you keep a gratitude journal? Well, good for you. That is certainly a great way to focus on the positives in your life. I find that an even more powerful way to have an attitude of gratitude is by living, eating, and breathing an attitude of gratitude. The way to do this is by focusing on EVERYTHING each day that you are grateful for. Yes, I mean EVERYTHING. From your health all the way down to having a toothbrush. If you do this for three months straight, your life will never be the same! You are going to begin to see ALL the good that is in your life and you will feel a sense of joy, happiness, and excitement unlike ever before!

After the three months are over, let your attitude of gratitude become a permanent part of your life. This will be one of the best gifts you can give yourself. You will find that after a few months, you will be pleasantly overwhelmed with gratitude at times. This is what happened to me. I am so glad that I live my life this way. I cannot begin to tell you how much joy and happiness I feel from focusing on everything that I am grateful for throughout each and every day. When I first started thinking about everything I was grateful for, I thought it was a little much for me to be grateful for small things. Then I realized that I was indeed grateful for the small things: without them my life would be more stressful.

Vanessa felt constantly worried and anxious because her best friend had cancer. Vanessa said that focusing on everything she was grateful for helped her to stay focused on the NOW. Therefore, she had a significant decrease in anxiety and worry about her best friend and the future. Vanessa mentioned that she is now able to take in all the good more than ever due to this technique. You, too, will experience amazing benefits from keeping track of everything you are grateful for throughout your day!

Do not put off this exercise. It will change your life forever! You may think that it is a waste of time to run through everything that you are grateful for each day. Becoming happier, more joyful, and excited about life will be worth all the time it takes to think about everything that you are grateful for! Give it a try!

When you feel good about yourself and follow your inner voice and your heart's desires, you will embrace all the good that is in store for you! The time to embrace this good is now! Give yourself the gift of being open to all the good that is in store for you and allow yourself to be grateful!

CHAPTER 17
Ask for What You Want

I have had amazing things happen to me simply by believing that I would have what I wanted and by taking action. I clearly remember a conversation I had with a former classmate the day I graduated from college. Claire asked me what I planned on doing in the future. I let her know that I wanted to continue with my education and earn my Master's in Social Work at Rutgers University. At that time, Rutgers was the only school in the state of New Jersey that offered a Master's degree in Social Work. Therefore, the program was very competitive. Claire adamantly said to me, "I have a friend who applied to that program last year. She is a straight-A student and she has been in the field for a couple of years. She did not get in the program, so you will not get in either." I could have let her comment completely discourage me to the point where I did not even apply to the program. But I did and I was accepted. Thank goodness I did not let someone else's doubt discourage me and stop me from having my heart's desire. It is so important to believe in yourself, so that discouragement from others holds no power over your life.

In addition to believing you will have what you want, your intentions need to be very specific, so that you can be drawn to do the precise things that you need to do in order to manifest what you want. Your intentions are powerful. I am often amazed by their power. Whenever I want something, I will get clear about what I want and before I know it, my intuition leads me to take the exact steps that I need to take in order to make what I want a reality. Get clear on your intentions. If you do not know what they are, then you are saying, "Oh, I will accept anything, regardless of whether or not this adds to my life." This is a scary thought! With that type of thinking, you might as well go to any restaurant in a foreign country and tell a stranger to order for you. I do not know about you, but this would not work for me. I like to order exactly what I want. The same is true in life; I love to place an order with life, so that I can savor every bite of my delicious outcome.

Samantha said that she always had the desire to write a book. We talked about her desire and what that meant to her. She wanted to write a book so that she could help others and fulfill her dream of becoming a writer. She was very specific about what she wanted. Before she specifically thought about her intentions, she simply had the dream of writing a book, without any clear direction. Once she identified her reasons for writing, this helped to motivate her to take action. Within two years, Samantha had published two books! If she did not get clear about what her intentions were and take the necessary steps to make her dreams come true, then her books never would have come to fruition. She would have simply had a dream.

Witnessing how your intentions manifest what you want can be lots of fun. For three years, I wanted an ebony baby grand piano that sounded great. I knew exactly how much I wanted to pay for my piano. I kept searching and searching for the right piano, but it was nowhere to be found. As doubt entered my mind, I started to question whether what I wanted was reasonable. Out of frustration one day, I almost purchased a new piano that would have completely wiped out my savings.

At my moment of high frustration, I doubted that I was ever going to get what I wanted since I had been searching for my piano for three years! What mainly stopped me from making that mistake was the expensive piano did not produce the exact sound I wanted. My piano teacher's feedback surely paid off in that moment. I immediately recalled her telling me that I have a really good ear for sound. If Sue had not told me this, I would have doubted that the sound I was hearing might not be what I wanted. Even though I was having trouble trusting that I was going to get what I wanted, my inner voice reminded me that I needed to be patient. Once I heard my inner voice speak, I told myself that I had to continue to trust and have faith that I was going to have what was in my heart at the perfect time.

One month after my high degree of frustration, I felt led to call about a baby grand piano that I saw on-line. I immediately called the owner of the piano, Gail. She told me that she and her family had just moved to New Jersey from Georgia and that her home was too small for their baby grand piano. Gail mentioned that she and her husband loved the piano. I have to say that I was annoyed that I had to drive an hour away with no guarantee that this piano was the right one. I knew I had to keep an open mind, so I pushed myself to take action and see it.

When I saw the piano, I thought it looked fabulous, just like all the other beautiful ebony pianos that were in perfect condition that I'd seen over the past three years. I knew that the real test was hearing how the piano sounded. The minute I sat down and played the piano, tears slowly rolled down my cheeks. My tears appeared to be in perfect harmony with every key that I played. Here I was playing the exact piano that I had envisioned three years earlier, at the exact price that I wanted to pay! That was an incredible moment in my life.

Gail told me that she and her husband had an appraiser look at the piano a week earlier and that the piano was worth much more than what they were asking. However, as long as the piano went to someone who would appreciate it, she and her husband agreed to sell it for much less than it was worth. I had chills run up and down my arms after I heard her say that. She also said that she could not wait to tell her husband how excited I was to buy their piano. Here I was beaming with joy, knowing that I'd just purchased the piano of my dreams, and Gail was telling me how happy she was that I was the person buying the piano. Wow! This was pretty amazing!

Even though I experienced frustration throughout the three years, I needed to keep positive and fully believe that I could receive exactly what I wanted. I am so glad that I did not give in to my frustration, because if I had purchased the more expensive piano, I would have suffered the consequences financially. Plus, I would have settled for something that I truly did not want. If I did not believe that what seemed impossible was possible, then this would have stopped me from taking action toward having exactly what I wanted.

If you do not get what you want right away, it is because the timing is not right. You need to keep positive and believe that you will receive what you want up until the very moment that you receive it. Keep in mind that if you do not get what you want, it is because there is something greater in store for you. Get very clear about what you want. Take a few minutes to describe what you want in as much detail as possible.

> *"Respect yourself. Listen to what you really want and follow your instincts—they are usually right."*
> *— Jerilyn Ross*

What I really want is:

_____

_____

_____

_____

> *"You can have anything you want if you want it desperately enough. You must want it with an inner exuberance that erupts through the skin and joins the energy that created the world."*
> *— Sheila Graham*

How would you feel about having all the things on your list? Take a few minutes to enjoy all the good feelings that come from having these things. If you are unable to say thank you in advance for receiving what you want, perhaps you have some beliefs that are blocking you from being open to having what you want. Examine what beliefs you need to get rid of, so that you can believe that you will receive what you want. If you do not feel worthy enough to receive what you want, then you have healing to do.

> *"Every moment of your life is infinitely creative*
> *and the universe is endlessly bountiful.*
> *Just put forth a clear enough request,*
> *and everything your heart desires must come to you."*
> — *Shakti Gawain*

You may be thinking that you cannot have what you want because then you will be taking something away from someone who is less fortunate. This limiting belief will get you nowhere. There is enough for everyone! The more you have, the more you will be able to give to others.

The more you focus on what you want, the more you will take the necessary steps to make this happen. Why not make a collage of everything you want? Look at your collage daily. Ask yourself, "What steps do I need to take in order to make everything on my collage a reality?" On top of my collage, I wrote that I wanted greater peace and joy. A month after I created my collage, my life slowly began to change and I was experiencing more peace and joy.

People often create their own agony over not getting what they want. If you have taken all the necessary steps to make what you want happen and you are still not getting the results you had hoped for, then you need to let go. Either the timing is off or this is not right for your life. It is important to make peace with this. Once you give up the struggle of trying to make something happen that is not right for you, then you will be back on track to experiencing inner peace.

Life is meant to be enjoyed. Once you believe that there is a great plan for your life, then you will give up the struggle. Being stuck in mud by focusing on feeling sorry for yourself for not having what you want does not do any good. You can easily make yourself miserable that way. There are people who have hardly anything and yet they stay focused with gratitude on what they do have. These people's lives are rich with peace and joy.

Feeling sorry for yourself for not having what you want will put you down Misery Lane. Turn your life vehicle around toward Faith and Trust Road. You will enjoy the scenery down these roads more than any other. Plus, fewer storms touch these roads. I have witnessed individuals who made other people's lives miserable since they did not have what they wanted. Once they got what they wanted, they continued to complain about not having more. They did not know how to get off Misery Lane no matter how much good they received. The way to get off Misery Lane is by appreciating and giving thanks for what you do have. The more grateful you are for what you have, the more you will enjoy those things, without pushing them to the side because you want more. Stop feeling sorry for yourself and be grateful for what you have.

People who lie, deceive, and hurt others fail to realize that they can get what they want without resorting to these behaviors and feeling terrible about themselves in the process. When your integrity is not in order, you cannot feel good about yourself. At any moment, you can make a commitment to stop doing things that keep you feeling terrible about yourself. When you really like who you are, then you will be FULLY open to creating the life of your dreams.

It is also important to ask others specifically for what you want and need. There are plenty of people in this world who will get great pleasure out of helping you. You may not always get what you are asking for; however, you have the right to ask anyway. No one can read your mind, so ask for what you want. If you are uncomfortable with asking for the big things you want, then start off small. As you get the results that you are looking for in small ways, this will help you to ask for those more important things that you want.

Just the other day, I was at a shoe store, where I always buy my favorite sneakers. The shoe store had a sale where you could buy one pair of sneakers at full price and get another pair half off. I love buying things on sale, so I was excited to take advantage of that offer. I found two pairs of sneakers that I really liked, but they had only one of them in my size. I convinced myself to just buy a bigger size for that one, since I really liked the sneakers. I figured that I could wear thicker socks. I then realized that I needed to ask for what I wanted, rather than settle. I asked the girl at the register if they had the size I needed, and she said that she was going to do a store search on her computer. I was told that they could order the sneakers for me and send them to my house for no additional charge! If I had not asked for what I wanted, I would have settled for something that was not right for me. This is a small example of how asking for what you want can bring great results.

Extraordinary people will continue to ask for what they want until they get it. Ordinary people will give up after they hear the word no. Good things will happen when you ask for what you want. How often do you ask others for what you want? Most people do not ask for what they want because they are afraid to hear the word no. They may feel rejected and discouraged when someone turns down their request. It is important to remember that one person's no may be another person's "yes." There were many times when I stopped myself from asking for what I truly wanted because I was afraid of being turned down. For me the word no used to mean that I was being rejected. What does the word no mean to you? Once I realized that the word no was not about me, it was about what I was asking, I no longer feared being turned down. Great freedom comes from not allowing the word "no" to stop you. One way to make this happen is by seeing that the word no is simply "no" to your request. You can ask a thousand people for what you want, and only one person may say "yes." All you need is that one "yes"!

You do not need to apologize for having what you want. There is plenty on this planet for everyone to have what they want. The more you allow yourself to receive what you want, the more joy you will experience. And everyone around you will benefit by being around someone who is happy, positive, and living a great life. Your happiness will be contagious to everyone and positively impact them!

Conclusion: Living an Extraordinary Life

Experiencing a severe crisis, trauma, or loss feels horrible. However, keep reminding yourself that your feelings are only TEMPORARY! Now that you are healing, you will benefit from that experience. Something good will come out of your difficult situation. You may already know some of the good. If not, allow yourself to focus on your good. Perhaps one positive thing is that you are now ready to create a better life than the one you had before.

Allow this book to continue to support you on your journey toward creating a happy life. Use it as a reference guide as you heal, grow, and evolve. Keep referring to what you have written and continue to write throughout your process. Even though your healing is temporary, most of the tools and techniques offered in this book can be used throughout your life. No matter where you are on your journey, know that there are people who care about you, even people you have never met. I am one of those people. I wish you a life filled with joy, peace, and happiness!

My hope is that this book has positively impacted your life and will help you to become healed and happy. You have the power within you to create the life of your dreams! Take one step at a time on this journey, and accept guidance along the way. Feel free to let me know how this book has impacted you at normalight@aol.com (Unfortunately, because of the large number of e-mails that I receive, I may not be able to respond to yours.) Perhaps one day we will meet in person. If you are interested in signing up for one of my seminars that will help you to heal and create an extraordinary life, please register on-line. I wish you much peace and happiness!

Compliment Journal

Over the next thirty days, write every compliment you receive from others in this journal. On the days when you do not receive a compliment, give one to yourself. Review this list often. This will surely help you feel good!

Compliments Received & Given to Myself

Day 1:

_____

_____

_____

Day 2:

_____

_____

_____

Day 3:

_____

_____

_____

Day 4:

_____

_____

_____

Compliments Received & Given to Myself

Day 5:

_____

_____

_____

Day 6:

_____

_____

_____

Day 7:

_____

_____

_____

Day 8:

_____

_____

_____

Day 9:

_____

_____

_____

Compliments Received & Given to Myself

Day 10:

Day 11:

Day 12:

Day 13:

Day 14:

Compliments Received & Given to Myself

Day 15:

Day 16:

Day 17:

Day 18:

Day 19:

Compliments Received & Given to Myself

Day 20:

_____
_____
_____

Day 21:

_____
_____
_____

Day 22:

_____
_____
_____

Day 23:

_____
_____
_____

Day 24:

_____
_____
_____

Day 25:

_____
_____
_____

Compliments Received & Given to Myself

Day 26:
_____
_____
_____

Day 27:
_____
_____
_____

Day 28:
_____
_____
_____

Day 29:
_____
_____
_____

Day 30:
_____
_____
_____

Day 31:
_____
_____
_____

The Compliments I received helped me to see that

Compliment Journal

The compliments I gave myself helped me to see that

My Compliment Journal helped me by